Last Judgment

Last Judgment
by Emanuel Swedenborg
Translated by John Whitehead

Start Publishing PD LLC
Copyright © 2024 by Start Publishing PD LLC

All rights reserved, including the right to reproduce this book or portions thereof in any form whatsoever.

Start Publishing PD is a registered trademark of Start Publishing PD LLC
Manufactured in the United States of America

Cover art: Shutterstock/Taisiya Kozorez

Cover design: Jennifer Do

10 9 8 7 6 5 4 3 2 1

ISBN 979-8-8809-0715-1

I. THE DESTRUCTION OF THE WORLD IS NOT MEANT BY THE DAY OF THE LAST JUDGMENT. Those who have not known the spiritual sense of the Word, have understood that everything in the visible world will be destroyed in the day of the Last Judgment; for it is said, that heaven and earth are then to perish, and that God will create a New Heaven and a New Earth. In this opinion they have also confirmed themselves because it is said, that all are then to rise from their graves, and that the good are then to be separated from the evil, with more to the same purport. But it is thus said in the sense of the letter of the Word, because the sense of the letter of the Word is natural, and in the ultimate of Divine order, where each and every part contains a spiritual sense within it. For which reason, he who comprehends the Word only according to the sense of the letter, may be led into various opinions, as indeed has been the case in the Christian world, where so many heresies have thus arisen, and every one of them is confirmed from the Word. But since no one has hitherto known, that in the whole and in every part of the Word there is a spiritual sense, nor even what the spiritual sense is, therefore they who have embraced this opinion concerning the Last Judgment are excusable. But still they may now know, that neither the visible heaven nor the habitable earth will perish, but that both will endure; and that by "the New Heaven and the New Earth" is meant a New Church, both in the heavens and on the earth. It is said a New Church in the heavens, for there is a church in the heavens, as well as on the earth; for there also is the Word, and likewise preachings, and Divine worship as on the earth; but with a difference, that there all things are in a more perfect state, because there they are not in the natural world, but in the spiritual; hence all there are spiritual men, and not natural as they were in the world. That it is so, may be seen in the work on Heaven, in a special article there, on the Conjunction of Heaven with man by the Word ; and on Divine Worship in Heaven.

The passages in the Word, in which mention is made of the destruction of heaven and earth, are the following: Lift up your eyes to heaven, and look upon the earth beneath; the heavens are about to perish like smoke, and the earth shall wax old like a garment (Isa. 51:6). Behold, I am about to create new heavens, and a new earth; neither shall the former things be remembered (Isa. 65:17). I will make new heavens and a new earth (Isa. 66:22). The stars of heaven have fallen to the earth, and heaven has departed like a book rolled together (Apoc. 6:13, 14). I saw a great throne, and One sitting thereon, from whose face the earth and the heaven fled away, and their place was not found (Apoc. 20:11). I saw a New Heaven and a New Earth, for the first heaven and the first earth had passed away (Apoc. 21:1). In these passages, by "a New Heaven" is not meant the visible heaven, but heaven itself where the human race is collected; for a heaven was formed from all the human race, who had lived since the commencement of the Christian church; but they who were there were not angels, but spirits of various religions; this heaven is meant by "the first heaven" which was to perish: but how this was, shall be specially declared in what follows; here is related only so much as serves to show what is meant by "the first heaven" which was to perish. Every one even who thinks from a somewhat enlightened reason, may perceive, that it is not the starry heaven, the so immense firmament of creation, which is here meant, but that it is heaven in the spiritual sense, where angels and spirits are.

That by "the new earth" is meant a New Church on earth, has hitherto been unknown, for every one by "earth" in the Word has understood the earth, when yet by it is meant the church; in the natural sense, earth is the earth, but in the spiritual sense it is the church, because they who are in the spiritual sense, that is, who are spiritual, as the angels are, when "the earth" is named in the Word, do not understand the earth itself, but the nation which is there, and its Divine worship; hence it is that by "earth" is signified the church; that it is so, may be seen in the Arcana Coelestia, as quoted below. I will here adduce one or two passages from the Word, by which in some measure it may be comprehended, that "earth" [land] signifies the church: The cataracts from on high were opened, and the foundations of the earth were shaken; in breaking, the earth is broken; in agitating, the earth is agitated; in reeling, the earth reels like a drunkard; it moves to and fro like a cottage; and heavy upon it is the transgression thereof (Isa. 24:18-20). I will cause a man to be more rare than pure gold; therefore I will remove the heaven, and the earth shall be removed out of her place, in the day of the fierce anger of Jehovah (Isa. 13:12, 13). The earth was agitated before Him, the heavens have trembled, the sun and the moon are become black, and the stars have withdrawn their splendor (Joel 2:10). The land was shaken and agitated, and the foundations of the mountains trembled and were shaken (Ps. 18:7, 8, and in many other places). FROM THE ARCANA

COELESTIA. By "earth" (land) in the Word is signified the kingdom of the Lord and the church). Chiefly for this reason, because by "earth" is meant the land of Canaan, and the church was there from the most ancient times hence also it is, that heaven is called the heavenly Canaan. And because in the spiritual sense by "earth" is understood the nation which is there, and its worship. Hence the "earth" signifies various things pertaining to the church. The people of the "earth" are they who are of the spiritual church. "An earthquake" is a change of the state of the church. "A New Heaven and a New Earth" signify the church. The Most Ancient Church, which was before the flood, and the Ancient Church, which was after the flood, were in the land of Canaan). Thence all the places there became representative of such things as are in the Lord's kingdom and in the church. Therefore Abraham was commanded to go thither, since with his posterity from Jacob, a representative church was to he instituted, and the word written, the ultimate sense of which should consist of the representatives and significatives which were there. Hence it is that by "earth" and by "the land of Canaan" is signified the church.

"To create" in the spiritual sense of the Word also signifies to form, to establish, and to regenerate; so by "creating a new heaven and a new earth" signifies to establish a New Church in heaven and on earth, as may appear from the following passages: The people who shall be created shall praise Jah (Ps. 102:18). Thou sendest forth the spirit, they are created; and Thou renewest the faces of the earth (Ps. 104:30). Thus said Jehovah, thy Creator, O Jacob, thy Former, O Israel, for I have redeemed thee, and I have called thee by thy name, thou art Mine; every one called by My name, and for My glory I have created, I have formed him, yea, I have made him (Isa. 43:1, 7, and in other places). Hence it is, that "the new creation" of man is his reformation, since he is made anew, that is, from natural he is made spiritual; and hence it is that "a new creature" is a reformed man. "To create" is to create anew, or to reform and regenerate. "To create a New Heaven and a New Earth," is to institute a new church. By "the creation of heaven and earth" in the first chapter of Genesis, in the internal sense, is described the institution of the celestial church, which was the Most Ancient Church.

Concerning the spiritual sense of the Word, see in the small work on the White Horse, mentioned in the Apocalypse.

II. THE PROCREATIONS OF THE HUMAN ON THE EARTHS WILL NEVER CEASE. They who have adopted as their belief concerning the Last Judgment, that all things in the heavens and on the earth are then to perish, and that a new heaven and a new earth will exist in their place, believe, because it follows of consequence, that the generations and procreations of the human race are therefore to cease. For they think that all things will be then accomplished, and that men will be in a different state from before. But since the day of the Last Judgment does not mean the destruction of the world, as was shown in the preceding article, it also follows that the human race will endure, and that procreations will not cease.

That the procreations of the human race will endure to eternity, is plain from many considerations, of which some are shown in the work on Heaven, especially from the following: I. The human race is the basis on which heaven is founded. II. The human race is the seminary of heaven. III. The extension of heaven, which is for angels, is so immense that it cannot be filled to eternity. IV. They are but few respectively, of whom heaven at present is formed. V. The perfection of heaven increases according to its numbers. VI. And every Divine work has respect to infinity and eternity.

I. The human race is the basis on which heaven is founded, is because man was last created, and that which is last created is the basis of all that precedes. Creation commenced from the supreme or inmost, because from the Divine; and proceeded to ultimates or extremes, and then first subsisted. The ultimate of creation is the natural world, including the terraqueous globe, with all things on it. When these were finished, then man was created, and into him were collated all things of Divine order from firsts to lasts; into his inmost were collated those things of that order which are primary; and into his ultimates those which are ultimate; so that man was made Divine order in form. Hence it is that all things in man and with man, are both from heaven and from the World, those of his mind from heaven, and those of his body from the world; for the things of heaven flow into his thoughts and affections, and dispose them according to reception by his spirit, and the things of the world flow into his sensations and pleasures, and dispose them according to reception in his body, but still in accommodation to their agreement with the thoughts and affections of his spirit. That it is so, may be seen in several articles in the work on Heaven and Hell, especially in the following: That the Whole Heaven, in one complex, has reference to one man; each society in the Heavens likewise); that hence every Angel is in a perfect human form; and that this is from the Divine Human of the Lord. And moreover under the article on the Correspondence of all things of Heaven with all things of Man. On the Correspondence of Heaven with all things on earth. And on the Form of Heaven. From this order of creation it may appear, that such is the binding chain of connection from firsts to lasts that all things together make one, in which the prior cannot be separated from the posterior (just as a cause cannot be separated from its effect); and that thus the spiritual world cannot be separated from the natural, nor the natural world from the spiritual; thence neither the angelic heaven from the human race, nor the human race from the angelic heaven. Wherefore it is so provided by the Lord, that each shall afford a mutual assistance to the other, that is, the angelic heaven to the human race, and the human race to the angelic heaven. Hence it is, that the angelic mansions are indeed in heaven, and to appearance separate from the mansions where men are; and yet they are with man in his affections of good and truth. Their presentation to sight, as separate, is from appearances; as may be seen in an article in the work on Heaven and Hell, where Space in Heaven is treated of. That the mansions of angels are with men in their affections of good and truth, is meant by these words of the Lord: He who loveth Me, keepeth my words, and my Father will love him, and we will come unto him, and make our mansion with him (John 14:23). By "the Father" and "the Lord" in the above passage is also meant heaven, for where the Lord is, there is heaven, since the Divine proceeding from the Lord makes heaven, as may be seen in the work on Heaven and Hell. And likewise by these words of the Lord: The Comforter the Spirit of Truth abideth with you, and is in you (John 14:17) "The Comforter" is the Divine truth proceeding from the Lord, for which reason He is also called "the Spirit of truth," and the Divine truth makes heaven, and also the angels, because they are recipients; that the Divine proceeding from the Lord is the Divine truth, and that the angelic heaven is from it, may be seen in the work on Heaven and Hell. The like is also understood by these words of the Lord: The kingdom of God is within you (Luke 17:21). "The kingdom of God" is the Divine good and truth, in which the angels are. That angels and spirits are with man, and in his affections, has been granted me to see a thousand times, from their presence and abode with me; but angels and spirits do not know with what men they are, neither do men know the angels and spirits they cohabit with, for the Lord alone knows and disposes this. In a word, there is an extension into heaven of all the affections of good and truth, and a communication and conjunction with those who are in the like affections there; and there is an extension into hell of all the affections of evil and falsity, and a communication and conjunction with these who are in the like affections there. The extension of the affections into the spiritual world, is almost like that of sight into the natural world; communications in both are nearly similar; yet with this difference, that in the natural world there are objects, but in the spiritual world angelic societies. Hence it appears, that the connection of the angelic heaven with the human race is such that the one subsists from the other, and that the angelic heaven without the human race would be like a house without a foundation, for heaven closes into it and rests upon it. The case herein is the same as with each particular man; his spiritual things, which pertain to his thought and will, inflow into his natural things, which pertain to his sensations and actions, and in these they terminate and subsist. If man were not in possession of them, that is, if he were without these boundings and ultimates, his spiritual things, which pertain to the thoughts and affections of his spirit, would flow away, like things unbounded, or like those which have no foundation. In like manner, when a man passes from the natural into the spiritual world, which takes place when he dies, then because he is a spirit, he no longer subsists on his own basis, but upon the common basis, which is the human race. He who knows not the arcana of heaven, may believe that angels subsist without men, and men without angels; but I can affirm from all my experience of heaven, and from all my discourse with the angels, that no angel or spirit subsists without man, and no man without spirits and angels, but that there is a mutual and reciprocal conjunction. From this, it may now be seen that the human race and the angelic heaven make one, and mutually and reciprocally subsist from each other, and thus that the one cannot be taken away from the other.

II. The human race is the seminary of heaven, will appear from a subsequent article, in which it will be shown, that heaven and hell are from the human race, and that therefore the human race is the seminary of heaven. It must, however, first be mentioned, that as heaven has been formed of the human race, from the first creation until now, so it will be formed and filled up from the same source hereafter. It is indeed possible that the human race on one earth may perish, which comes to pass when they separate themselves entirely from the Divine, for then man no longer has spiritual life, but only natural, like that of beasts; and when man is such no society can be formed, and held bound by laws, since without the influx of heaven, and thus without the Divine government, man would become insane, and rush unchecked into every wickedness, one against another. But although the human race, by separation from the Divine, might perish on one earth, which, however, is provided against by the Lord, yet still they would continue on other earths; for that there are earths in the universe to some hundreds of thousands, may be seen in the little work, The Earths in our Solar System called Planets, and the Earths in the Starry Heaven. It was said to me from heaven, that the human race on this earth would have perished, so that not one man would have existed on it at this day, if the Lord had not come into the world, and on this earth assumed the Human, and made it Divine; and also, unless the Lord had given here such a Word as might serve for a basis to the angelic heaven, and for its conjunction. That the conjunction of heaven with man is by the Word, may be seen in the work on Heaven and Hell. But that such is the case can be comprehended only by those who think spiritually, that is, by those who through the acknowledgment of the Divine in the Lord are conjoined with heaven, for they alone are able to think spiritually.

III. The extension of heaven, which is for angels, is so immense, that it cannot be filled to eternity, appears from what has been said in the work on Heaven and Hell. On the Immensity of Heaven ; and That they are, but few respectively of whom heaven is at present formed, in the little work on the Earths in the Universe.

IV. The perfection of heaven increases according to its numbers, is evident from its form, according to which its associations are disposed in order, and its communications flow, for it is the most perfect of all; and in proportion to the increase of numbers in that most perfect form, there is given a direction and consent of more and more to unity, and therefore a closer and a more unanimous conjunction; the consent and the conjunction derived from it increase from numbers, for everything is there inserted as a mediate relation between two or more, and what is inserted confirms and conjoins. The form of heaven is like the form of the human mind, the perfection of which increases according to the increase of truth and good, from whence are its intelligence and wisdom. The form of the human mind, which is in heavenly wisdom and intelligence, is like the form of heaven, because the mind is the least image of that form; hence it is, that on all sides there is a communication of the thoughts and affections of good and truth in such men, and in angels, with surrounding societies of heaven; and an extension according to the increase of wisdom, and thus according to the plurality of the knowledges of truth implanted in the intellect and according to the abundance of the affections of good implanted in the will; and therefore in the mind, for the mind consists of the intellect and the will. The human and angelic mind is such that it may be infilled to eternity, and as it is infilled, so it is perfected; and this is especially the case, when man is led by the Lord, for he is then introduced into genuine truths, which are implanted in his intellect, and into genuine goods, which are implanted in his will, for the Lord then disposes all things of such a mind into the form of heaven, until at length it is a heaven in the least form. From this comparison, which is a true parallel, it is evident, that the increasing number of the angels perfects heaven. Moreover, every form consists of various parts; a form which does not consist of various parts, is not a form, for it has no quality, and no changes of state; the quality of every form results from the arrangement of various things within it, from their mutual relation, and from their consent to unity, from which every form is considered as one; such a form, in proportion to the multitude of the various things arranged within it, is the more perfect, for every one of them, as was said above, confirms, corroborates, conjoins, and so perfects. But this is still more evident from what has been shown in the work on Heaven and Hell, especially where it treats of this: That every Society of Heaven is a Heaven in a lesser form, and every Angel a heaven in the least form ; and also in the article, On the Form of Heaven, according to which Consociations and Communications have place there ; and On the Wisdom of the Angels of Heaven.

V. Every Divine work has respect to infinity and eternity, is evident from many things which exist both in heaven and in the world: in neither of them is there ever given one thing exactly similar to, or the same as, another: no two faces are either alike or identical, nor will be to eternity: in like manner the mind of one is never altogether like that of another; wherefore there are as many faces and as many minds as there are men and angels. There never exists in any one man (in whom yet there are innumerable parts which constitute his body, and innumerable affections which constitute his mind) any one thing quite alike, or identical with any one thing in another man; hence it is that every one leads a life distinct from the life of another. The same order exists in the whole and in every part of nature. That such infinite variety is in each and in all, is because they all originate from the Divine, which is infinite; hence there is a certain image of infinity everywhere, to the end that the Divine may regard all things as His own work, and at the same time, that all things, as His work, may have respect to the Divine. A familiar instance may serve to illustrate the manner in which every thing in nature has respect to infinity and eternity. Any seed, be it the produce of a tree, or of grain, or of a flower, is so created, that it may be multiplied to infinity, and endure to eternity. For from one seed are produced many, five, ten, twenty, a hundred, and from each of these again as many more; such fructification from one seed continuing but for a century, would cover the surface not only of one, but of myriads of earths, the same seeds are so created, that their durations may be eternal. Hence it is evident, how the idea of infinity and eternity is in them; and the like is true in all other cases. The angelic heaven is the end for which all things in the universe were created, for it is the end on account of which the human race exists, and the human race is the end regarded in the creation of the visible heaven, and the earths included in it. Where fore that Divine work, namely, the angelic heaven, primarily has respect to infinity and eternity, and therefore to its multiplication without end, for the Divine Himself dwells therein. Hence also it is clear, that the human race will never cease, for were it to cease, the Divine work would be limited to a certain number, and thus its looking to infinity would perish.

    III. HEAVEN AND HELL ARE FROM THE HUMAN RACE. It is altogether unknown in the Christian world that heaven and hell are from the human race; for it is believed that angels were created at the beginning, and that heaven was formed of them; and that the Devil or Satan was an angel of light, who, becoming rebellions, was cast down with his crew, and that this was the origin of hell. The angels are greatly astonished at such a faith in the Christian world, and still more, that nothing at all is there known of heaven, when yet it is a primary doctrine in the church; and since such ignorance prevails, they are rejoiced in heart that it has now pleased the Lord to reveal to men many things concerning heaven, and also concerning hell; and by this means, as far as possible, to dissipate the darkness which daily increases, because the church has come to its end. Wherefore they wish me to declare from them, that there is in the universal heaven not one who was created an angel from the first, nor any devil in hell who was created an angel of light, and cast down, but that all both in heaven and in hell are from the human race; in heaven those who had lived in the world in heavenly love and faith, and in hell those who had lived in infernal love and faith; and that hell in the whole complex is called the Devil and Satan; that the hell behind, where those are who are called evil genii, is the Devil, and the hell in front, which is the abode of evil spirits, is Satan. What the nature of one hell is, and what the other, may be seen in the work on Heaven and Hell, towards the end. The angels said, that the Christian world have conceived such a belief about those in heaven and hell, from certain passages in the Word no otherwise understood than according to the sense of the letter, and not illustrated and explained by genuine doctrine from the Word; when yet the sense of the letter, if the genuine doctrine of the church does not shine before it, draws the mind away into various opinions; whence come ignorance, heresies, and errors. The hells, or the infernals, taken together, are called the Devil and Satan. They who have been devils in the world, become devils after death. The doctrine of the church must be from the Word. The Word is not understood without doctrine. True doctrine is a lamp to those who read the Word. Genuine doctrine must be from those who are in illustration from the Lord. They who are in the sense of the letter of the Word without doctrine, can come into no understanding of Divine truths. And they are led into many errors. The difference between those who teach and learn from the doctrine of the church from the Word, and those who teach and learn only from the sense of the letter of the word.

Another cause of such a belief in the man of the church is, that he believes that no one can go to heaven or hell before the time of the Last Judgment; of which he has conceived this opinion that the visible world is then to perish, and a new one will come into existence, and that then the soul will return into its body, and from their conjunction man will again live a man. This belief involves another about the angels, that they were created from the beginning; for it is impossible to believe that heaven and hell are from the human race, when it is believed that no man goes there till the end of the world. But in order that man may be convinced that it is not so, it has been granted me to have fellowship with angels, and also to speak with those who are in hell, and this now for many years, sometimes continuously from morning even to evening, and thus to be informed concerning heaven and hell; to the end that the man of the church may no longer remain in his erroneous belief, about a resurrection at the day of judgment, about a state of the soul in the interval, as well as about angels, and about the Devil; which belief, since it is a belief in falsity, induces darkness; and with those who think of such things from their own intelligence, brings on doubt, and at length denial; for they say in heart, how can so vast a heaven, and so many stars, with sun and moon, be destroyed and dissipated? and how can the stars fall from heaven upon the earth, which yet are larger than the earth? and how can bodies, eaten up by worms, consumed by putrefaction, and scattered to all the winds, be collected again for its own soul? in the meantime, where is the soul, and what is it without the senses which it had in the body? with such like sayings on matters, which being incomprehensible, fall not within belief, and destroy in many the faith in man's eternal life, in heaven and hell, and with them, in all the remaining things of the faith of the church. That faith has thus been destroyed is evident from those who say, Who ever came from heaven and told us that it exists? What is hell? Is it anything at all? What is the meaning of man's being tormented with fire to eternity? What is the day of judgment? Has it not been expected for ages in vain? and many more questions which involve a denial of all things. Lest therefore, they who think thus (as do many who, from their knowledge in worldly matters are reputed skilful and learned), should any longer disturb and seduce the simple in faith and heart, and induce infernal darkness concerning God, heaven, eternal life, and other subjects dependent upon these, the interiors of my spirit have been opened by the Lord, and thus it has been granted one to speak with all those of the deceased whom I ever knew in the life of the body, with some for days, with some for months, and with some for a year, and also with so many others, that I should come short if I reckoned them at an hundred thousand, of whom many were in the heavens, and many in the hells. I have also spoken with some two days after their decease, and told them that solemn preparations were then making for their funerals; to which they said, that it was well to reject that which had served them for a body and its functions in the world: and they desired me to say that they are not dead, but alive and equally men as before, and that they had only passed out of one world into another; and they did not know that they had lost anything, since they are in a body and its senses as before, and in intellect and will as before, and have like thoughts and affections, like sensations, pleasures, and desires, as in the world. Most of those newly deceased, when they saw that they were living men as before, and in a similar state (for after death the state of every one's life is at first similar to what it was in the world, but is successively changed with him either into heaven or into hell), were affected with new joy at being alive, and said that they had not believed this. But they greatly wondered that they had been in such ignorance and blindness concerning the state of their own lives after death; and more especially, that the man of the church is in such a state, when yet he of all in the world can be in light concerning them. Then for the first time they saw the cause of this blindness and ignorance, which is, that external things, which are worldly and corporeal, had occupied and filled their minds to such an extent, that they could not be elevated into the light of heaven and behold the things of the church, which are beyond its doctrinals. For mere darkness inflows from corporeal and worldly things, when they are so much loved as they are at the present day, when man wishes to think of the things of heaven, beyond the dictate of the doctrine of faith of his church. At this day few in Christendom believe that man rises again immediately after death, Pref. to chap. 16 of Gen. and. But at the time of the Last judgment, when the visible world is to perish. The cause of such belief. Nevertheless man does rise again immediately after death, and that then he is a man as to each and all things. The soul, which lives after death, is man's spirit, which is the real man in the man, and which also in the other life is in a perfect human form. The same from experience. And from the word. What in meant by the dead being seen in the holy city (Matt. xxvii. 53) is explained (. How man is raised from the dead; by experience. Of his state after resuscitation. False opinions about the soul and the resurrection.

Very many of the learned from the Christian world are amazed when they see themselves after death in a body, in garments, and in houses as they were in the world; and when they recall to memory what they had thought of the life after death, of the soul, of spirits, of heaven and of hell, they are affected with shame, declare that they have thought foolishly, and that the simple in faith are much wiser than they. The learned were explored, who had confirmed themselves in such things, and who had attributed all things to nature, and it was found, that the interiors of their minds were closed, and the exteriors opened, so that they had not looked to heaven, but to the world, and hence also to hell; for so far as the interiors of the mind are opened, so far man looks to heaven; but so far as the interiors are closed, and the exteriors opened, so far he looks to hell; for the interiors of man are formed for the reception of all things of heaven, and his exteriors for the reception of all things of the world, and they who receive the world, and not at the same time heaven, receive hell. In man the spiritual and the natural worlds are conjoined. Man's internal is formed in the image of heaven, but his external in the image of the world.

That the spirit of man, after its release from the body, is a man, and in a similar form, has been attested to me by the daily experience of many years; for I have seen, heard, and spoken with spirits a thousand times; and even on this very subject; that men in the world do not believe them to be such, that they who do believe it, are accounted as simple by the learned. The spirits were grieved in heart, that such ignorance should still prevail in the world, and most of all in the church; but this, they said, proceeded principally from the learned, who thought of the soul from the sensual corporeal; wherefore they have conceived no other idea of it, than as of mere thought; which, when it is regarded without any subject in which and from which it is viewed, is like some volatile form of pure ether, which is necessarily dispersed when the body dies. But since the church from the Word believes in the immortality of the soul, they were obliged to ascribe it to some vital quality, such as belongs to thought, though not the sensation which man has, till it is again conjoined to its body. On this opinion is founded the doctrine of the resurrection at the time of the Last Judgment, and a belief in the conjunction of the soul and the body then; for from this hypothesis about the soul, coupled with the belief of the church in man's eternal life, no other conclusion can be reached: hence it is, that when any one thinks of the soul, from the doctrine and the hypothesis together, he does not at all comprehend that it is a spirit, and that this is in the human form. Add to this, that scarcely any one at this day knows what the spiritual is, and still less that they who are spiritual, as all spirits and angels are, have any human form. Hence it is, that almost all who come from the world are greatly amazed that they are alive, and are equally men as before, with no difference whatever. But when they cease to be amazed at themselves, they then wonder that the church knows nothing of this state of men after death, when yet all who have ever lived in the world, are in the other life, and live as men. And because they have also wondered why this was not manifested to man by visions, it was told them from heaven, that this could be done, for nothing is easier, when the Lord pleases, but that still they who had confirmed themselves in falsities against it, would not believe, even though they themselves were to see it; and moreover that it is perilous to manifest anything from heaven to those who are in worldly and corporeal things, for in this case they would first believe and afterwards deny, and thus profane the very truth itself; for to believe and afterwards to deny, is to profane; and they who profane, are thrust down into the lowest and most grievous of all the hells. It is this danger which is meant by these words of the Lord: He hath blinded their eyes, and hardened their hearts, lest they should see with the eyes and understand with the heart; and convert themselves, and I should heal them (John 12:40). Also that they who are in worldly and corporeal loves, still would not believe, is meant by these words: Abraham said to the rich man in hell, They have Moses and the prophets, let them hear them; but he said, Nay, father Abraham, but if one from the dead come to them, they will be converted; but Abraham said to him, if they hear not Moses and the prophets, neither will they believe even if one rose from the dead (Luke 16:29-31).

That heaven is from the human race, is evident from this, that angelic and human minds are similar; both enjoying the faculty of understanding, of perceiving, and of willing; both being formed for receiving heaven. For the human mind possesses wisdom as well as the angelic; but it is not so wise in the world, because it is in a terrestrial body, in which its spiritual mind thinks naturally, for its spiritual thought, which it has in common with an angel, then flows down into the natural ideas corresponding with the spiritual, and is thus perceived in them. But it is otherwise when the mind of man is freed from its connection with the body; then it no longer thinks naturally but spiritually; and when spiritually it then thinks what is incomprehensible and ineffable to the natural man, as an angel does. Hence it is evident, that man's internal, which is called his spirit, in its essence is an angel. That an angel is in a perfect human form, may be seen in the work on Heaven and Hell: but when man's internal is not opened above, but only below, then still, after its removal from the body, it is in a human form, but a direful and diabolical one, for it cannot look upwards to heaven, but only downwards to hell. There are as many degrees of life in man, as there are heavens, and they are opened after death according to his life. Heaven is in man. The men who are living a life of love and charity, have angelic wisdom in them, but that it is then latent, and that they come into it after death. In the Word, the man who receives the good of love and of faith from the Lord, is called an angel.

That heaven and hell are from the human race, the church moreover might have known from the Word, and made it a part of its doctrine, if it had admitted enlightenment from heaven, and had attended to the Lord's words to the robber, that: Today he should be with Him in paradise (Luke 23:43); and to those which the Lord spake concerning the rich man and Lazarus, that: The one went to hell, and spoke thence with Abraham, and that the other went to heaven (Luke 16:19-31). Also to what the Lord told the Sadducees respecting the resurrection, that: God is not the God of the dead, but of the living (Matt. 22:32). And furthermore they might have known it from the common faith of all who live well, especially from their faith in the hour of death, when they are no longer in worldly and corporeal things, in that they believe they will go to heaven, as soon as the life of their body departs. This faith prevails with all, so long as they do not think, from the doctrine of the church, of a resurrection at the time of the Last Judgment. Inquire into the subject and you will be confirmed that it is so.

He who has been instructed concerning Divine order, may moreover understand, that man was created to become an angel, because in him is the ultimate of order, in which ultimate, whatever belongs to celestial and angelic wisdom may be formed, renewed, and multiplied. Divine order never subsists in the mediate, so as to form anything there without an ultimate, for it is not in its own fullness and perfection, but it proceeds to the ultimate. But when it is in its ultimate, it then forms, and also by mediates there collated, renews and produces itself farther, which is effected by procreations; wherefore the seminary of heaven is there. This also is meant by the things related of man, and of his creation in the first chapter of Genesis: God said, Let us make man in our image, according to our likeness; and God created man in His image, in the image of God created He him; male and female created He them; and God blessed them, and God said unto them, be fruitful and multiply. "To create in the image of God, and in the likeness of God," is to confer upon man all things of Divine order from firsts to ultimates, and thus to make him an angel as to the interiors of his mind.

That the Lord rose again not only as to the Spirit, but also as to the Body, is because the Lord, when He was in the world, glorified His whole Human, that is, made it Divine. For the soul, which He had from the Father, was the Divine Itself from Himself, and the body was made a similitude of the soul, that is of the Father, and therefore also Divine. Hence it is that He Himself, unlike any man, rose again as to both; which He also manifested to His disciples, who believed they saw a spirit when they saw Him; for he said: Behold My hands and My feet, that it is I Myself: feel Me and see, for a spirit has not flesh and bones, as ye see Me have (Luke 24:36-39). By which He pointed out that He was not only Man as to the Spirit, but also as to the body. Man rises again as to the spirit only. The Lord alone rose as to the body also.

Moreover that heaven and hell are from the human race, has been shown in many articles in the work on Heaven and Hell as in the following: Of the Nations and People in Heaven who are out of the Church. Of Infants in Heaven. Of the Wise and the Simple in Heaven. Of the Rich and the Poor in Heaven. Every Man is a Spirit, as regards his own interiors. Man after Death is in a perfect human Form. Man after Death is in all the sense, memory, thought, and affection, which he had in the world, and leaves nothing but his terrestrial body. Of the First state of man after Death. Of the Second State of man after Death. Of his Third state. See moreover what is said of the Hells. From all these articles it may be seen, that heaven does not consist of any angels created in the beginning, nor hell of any devil and his crew, but solely of those who have been born men.

IV. ALL WHO HAVE BEEN BORN MEN FROM THE BEGINNING OF CREATION, AND ARE DECEASED, ARE EITHER IN HEAVEN OR IN HELL. I. This follows from what has been said and shown in the preceding article, namely, that heaven and hell are from the human race. II. And from this, that every man after the life in the world, lives to eternity. III. Thus all who have ever been born men from the creation of the world, and are deceased, are either in heaven or in hell. IV. Since all who will be born hereafter, will also come into the spiritual world, that world is so vast, and is such that the natural world, in which are men on earth, cannot be compared with it. But in order that all these things may be the more distinctly perceived, and more plainly evident, I will expound and describe them one by one.

I. That all who have ever been born men from the beginning of creation, and are deceased, are either in heaven or in hell, follows from those things which have been said and shown in the preceding article, namely, that heaven and hell are from the human race. This is clear without explanation. It has been the common belief hitherto, that men will not come into heaven or into hell before the day of the Last Judgment, when souls will return into their own bodies, and thus to enjoy such things as are believed to belong only to the body. The simple have been led into this belief by men professing wisdom, who have investigated the interior state of man. Because these have thought nothing concerning the spiritual world, but only of the natural world, nor therefore of the spiritual man, they have not known that the spiritual man which is in every natural man, is in the human form, as well as the natural man. Hence it never entered their minds that the natural man draws his own human form from his spiritual man; although they might have seen that the spiritual man acts at will upon the whole, and upon every part of the natural man, and that the natural man of himself does nothing at all. It is the spiritual man who thinks and wills, for this the natural man of himself cannot do; and thought and will are the all in all of the natural man; for the natural man acts as the spiritual man wills, and also speaks as the spiritual thinks, and that so entirely, that action is nothing but will, and speech is nothing but thought, for on the removal of thought and will, speech and action cease in a moment. From this it is evident that the spiritual man is truly a man, and that he is in the whole, and in every part of the natural man, and that therefore their effigies are alike, for the part or particle of the natural man, in which the spiritual does not act, does not live. But the spiritual man cannot appear to the natural man, for the natural cannot see the spiritual, but the spiritual can see the natural; for this is according to order, but the converse is contrary to order; since there is given an influx, and therefore also a sight, of the spiritual into the natural, for sight too is influx, but not the reverse. It is the spiritual man who is called the spirit of man, and who appears in the spiritual world in a perfect human form, and lives after death. Because they who are intelligent have not known anything of the spiritual world, and therefore nothing of the spirit of man, as was said above, they have conceived therefore an idea that man cannot live a man, before his soul returns into the body, and again puts on the senses. Hence have arisen such vain ideas about man's resurrection, namely, that bodies, though eaten up by worms and fish, or entirely fallen to dust, are to be collected again by the Divine omnipotence, and re-united to souls; and that this is not to happen till the end of the world, when the visible universe is to perish; with many more like ideas, which are every one of them inconceivable, and at the first glance of the mind, strike it as impossible, and contrary to Divine order, tending thus to weaken the faith of many; for those who think wisely, cannot believe what they do not in some measure comprehend; and belief in impossibilities is not given, that is, a belief in such things as man thinks to be impossible. Hence also those who disbelieve the life after death, derive an argument in support of their denial. But that man rises again immediately after his decease, and that then he is in a perfect human form, may be seen in the work on Heaven and Hell, in many of its articles. These things have been said, that it may be still more confirmed that heaven and hell are from the human race, from which it follows, that all who were ever born men from the beginning of creation, and are deceased, are either in heaven or in hell.

II. That every man after the life in the world lives to eternity, is evident from this, that man is then spiritual, and no longer natural, and that the spiritual man, separated from the natural, remains such as he is to eternity, for man's state cannot be changed after death. Moreover, the spiritual of every man is in conjunction with the Divine, since it can think of the Divine, and also love the Divine, and be affected with all things which are from the Divine, such as those which the church teaches, and therefore it can be conjoined to the Divine by thought and will, which are the two faculties of the spiritual man, and constitute his life; and that which can thus be conjoined to the Divine, can never die, for the Divine is with it, and conjoins it to Himself. Man is also created to the form of heaven as to his mind, and the form of heaven is from the Divine itself, as may be seen in the work on Heaven and Hell, where it has been shown, That the Divine of the Lord makes and forms Heaven. That Man is created to be a Heaven in the least form. That Heaven in the whole complex, has reference to one Man. That hence an Angel is in a perfect human Form ; an angel is a man as to his spiritual. On this subject moreover, I have often spoken with the angels, who wondered exceedingly, that of those who are called intelligent in the Christian world, and who also are believed by others to be intelligent, there are very many who utterly reject the belief in their own immortality, believing that the soul of man is dissipated at death, just as the soul of a beast is; not perceiving the distinction between the life of a man and the life of a beast; that man has the power of thinking above himself, of God, of heaven, of love, of faith, of good, spiritual and moral, of truths, and the like, and that thus he may be elevated to the Divine itself, and he conjoined by all those things to Him; but that beasts cannot be elevated above their own natural, to think of such things, and consequently that their spiritual cannot be separated from their natural after death, so as to live by itself, as man's spiritual can: whence also it is, that the life of a beast ceases on the dissipation of its natural life. The reason why many of the stalled intelligent in the Christian world, have no belief in the immortality of their own lives, the angels declared to be this, that in heart they deny the Divine, and acknowledge nature instead of the Divine; and they who think from such principles, are not able to think of any eternity by conjunction with the Divine, nor consequently, of the state of man as dissimilar to that of beasts, for in rejecting the

Divine from thought, they also reject eternity. They declared moreover, that with every man there is an inmost or supreme degree of life, or an inmost or supreme something into which the Divine of the Lord proximately inflows, and from which He disposes all the remaining interiors belonging to the spiritual and natural man, which are successive in both according to the degrees of order. This inmost or supreme they called the Lord's entrance into man, and His veriest dwelling place with him; and they said, that by this inmost or supreme, man is man, and is distinguished from brute animals which do not have it; and that hence it is, that men, as regards the interiors which are of the mind and disposition, unlike animals, can be elevated by the Lord to Himself, can have faith in Him, be affected by love to Him, and can receive intelligence and wisdom, and speak from reason. When I asked them concerning those who day the Divine, and the Divine truths, by which the conjunction of the life of man with the Divine itself is effected, and who yet live to eternity, they replied, that these also have the faculty of thinking and of willing, and therefore of believing and loving the things which are from the Divine, as well as those who acknowledge the Divine, and that by this faculty, they too live to eternity; they added, that this faculty is from that inmost or supreme which is in every man, of which mention was made above; that even those who are in hell have that faculty, and that they derive from it the power of reasoning and speaking against Divine truths, has been shown in many places. Hence it is, that every man lives to eternity, whatever be his quality. Because every man after death lives to eternity, no angel or spirit ever thinks of death; indeed they do not at all know what it is to die; wherefore, when "death" is mentioned in the Word, the angels understand by it either damnation, which is death in the spiritual sense, or the continuation of life and the resurrection. These things have been said in confirmation that all the men who have ever been born, and have died, from the beginning of creation, are alive, some in heaven, and some in hell. There is also an influx from the spiritual world into the lives of beasts, but that it is general, and not special as with man. The distinction between men and beasts is, that men can be elevated above themselves to the Lord, can think of the Divine, love it, and may thus be conjoined to the Lord, whence they have eternal life; but it is otherwise with beasts, which cannot be elevated to such things. When "death" is mentioned in the word, and spoken of the wicked, in heaven are understood damnation, which is spiritual death, and also hell. They who are in goods and truths are called "living," but they who are in evils and falsities "dead". By "death," when spoken of the good who die, resurrection and continuation of life are understood in heaven, for at death man rises again, continues his own life, and advances in it to eternity.

III. In order that I might know that all who have ever been born men from the beginning of creation, and are deceased, are either in heaven or in hell, it has been granted me to speak with some who lived before the flood; and also with some who lived after the flood; and with certain of the Jewish nation, who are made known to us from the Word of the Old Testament; with some who lived in the Lord's time; with many who lived in the ages succeeding, even down to the present day; and moreover with all those of the dead, whom I had known during their lives in the body; and likewise with infants; and with many of the Gentiles. From this experience I have been fully convinced, that there is not even one, who was ever born a man, from the first creation of this earth, who is not in heaven or in hell.

IV. Because all, who are to be born hereafter, must also come into the spiritual world, that world is so vast and such, that the natural world, in which men are on earth, cannot be compared with it; this is evident from the immense multitude of men who have passed into the spiritual world since the first creation, and who are together there; as well as from the continual increase hereafter from the human race, which will be added to them, and this without end, according to what has been shown above, in an article for the purpose , namely, that the procreations of the human race on the earths will never cease. When my eyes have been opened, it has sometimes been granted me to see how immense, even now, is the multitude of men who are there; it is so great that it can scarcely be numbered, such myriads are there, and this only in one place, towards one quarter; what then must the numbers be in the other quarters? For all are there collected into societies, and the societies exist in vast numbers, and each society, in its own place, forms three heavens, and three hells under them; wherefore there are some who are on high, some who are in the middle, and some who are below them; and underneath, there are those who are in the lowest places, or in the hells; and those who are above dwell among themselves as men dwell in cities, in which hundreds of thousands are together. Whence it is evident, that the natural world, the abode of men on earth, cannot be compared with that world, as regards the multitude of the human race; so that when man passes from the natural world into the spiritual, it is like going from a village into a great city. That the natural world cannot be compared with the spiritual world as to quality, may appear from this, that not only have all the things which are in the natural world an existence there, but innumerable others besides, which never were seen in this world, nor can be presented to the sight, for spiritual things there are effigied each to its own type by appearances, as if natural, each with an infinite variety; for the spiritual so far exceeds the natural in excellence, that the things are few which can be produced to the natural sense; the natural sense not receiving one of the thousands which the spiritual mind receives; and all things which belong to the spiritual mind, are presented, even in forms to their sight. This is the reason why it is impossible to describe what the spiritual world is, as regards its magnificent and stupendous things. These moreover increase in proportion to the multiplication of the human race in the heavens, for all things are there presented in forms which correspond to the state of each as to love and faith, and thence as to intelligence and wisdom; thus with a variety which increases continually, as the multitude increases. Whence it has been said by those who have been elevated into heaven, that they saw and heard things there, which no eye has ever seen, and no ear has ever heard. From these things, it may appear that the spiritual world is such, that the natural world can not be compared with it. Moreover, what it is, may be seen in the work on Heaven and Hell, where it treats of the two Kingdoms of Heaven. Of the Societies of Heaven Of representatives and Appearances in Heaven. Of the Wisdom of the Angels of Heaven. The things there described, however, are very few.

V. THE LAST JUDGMENT MUST BE WHERE ALL ARE TOGETHER, THUS IN THE SPIRITUAL WORLD, AND NOT ON EARTH. Concerning the Last Judgment, it is believed that the Lord will then appear in the clouds of heaven with the angels in glory, and awaken from the sepulchers all who have ever lived since the beginning of creation, clothing their souls with their bodies; and thus summoned together He will judge them, those who have done well, to eternal life or heaven, those who have done ill, to eternal death or hell. The churches derive this belief from the sense of the letter of the Word, nor could it be removed, so long as men did not know that there is a spiritual sense within each thing which is said in the Word, and that this sense is the Word itself, to which the sense of the letter serves for a foundation or basis, and that without such a letter, the Word could not have been Divine, or have served in heaven, as in the world, for the doctrine of life and faith, and for conjunction. He therefore who knows the spiritual things corresponding to the natural things in the Word, can know that by "the Lord's coming in the clouds of heaven," is not meant such an appearance of Him, but His appearance in the Word; for "the Lord" is the Word, because He is the Divine truth; "the clouds of heaven" in which He is to come, are the sense of the letter of the Word, and "the glory" is its spiritual sense; "the angels" are the heaven from which He will appear, and they also are the Lord as to Divine truths. Hence the meaning of these words is now evident, namely, that when the end of the church is, the Lord will open the spiritual sense of the Word, and thus the Divine truth, such as it is in itself; therefore that this is the sign that the Last Judgment is at hand. That there is a spiritual sense within each thing and expression in the Word, and what it is may be seen in the Arcana Coelestia, in which each and all things of Genesis and Exodus are explained according to that sense; and a collection of passages extracted from it, concerning the Word and its spiritual sense, may be seen in the little work on The White Horse, Mentioned in the Apocalypse. The Lord is the Word, because He is the Divine truth in heaven. The Lord is the Word, also because it is from Him, and treats of Him ; and because it treats of the Lord alone, and primarily of the glorification of His Human in its inmost sense, so that the Lord Himself is therein. The coming of the Lord is His presence in the Word, and revelation. "Clouds" in the Word signify the Word in the letter, or the sense of its letter. "Glory in the Word signifies Divine truth, such as it is in heaven, and such as it is in the spiritual sense. "Angels" in the Word signify Divine truths from the Lord, since angels are receptions of them, and do not speak them from themselves, but from the Lord. "Trumpets" or "cornets," which the angels then have, signify Divine truths in heaven and revealed from heaven).

That the Last Judgment must be in the spiritual world, and not in the natural world, or on the earth, is evident from the two preceding articles, and also from those that follow. In the two preceding articles it has been shown, that heaven and hell are from the human race; and that all who were ever born men since the beginning of creation, and are deceased, are either in heaven or in hell, thus that all are there together; but in the articles which follow it shall be shown that the Last Judgment has already been accomplished.

Moreover, no one is judged from the natural man, thus not so long as he lives in the natural world, for man is then in a natural body; but every one is judged in the spiritual man, and therefore when he comes into the spiritual world, for man is then in a spiritual body. It is the spiritual in man which is judged, but not the natural, for this cannot be held guilty of any fault or crime, since it does not live of itself, but is only the servant, and instrument by which the spiritual man acts. Hence also it is, that judgment is effected upon men when they have put off their natural, and put on their spiritual bodies. In the spiritual body moreover, man appears such as he is with respect to love and faith, for every one in the spiritual world is the effigy of his own love, not only as to the face and the body, but also as to the speech and the actions (see the work on Heaven and Hell,. Hence it is, that the qualities of all are known, and they are immediately separated, whenever the Lord pleases. From what has been said it is plain, that judgment is effected in the spiritual world, but not in the natural world, or on the earth.

That the natural life in man effects nothing, but his spiritual life in the natural, since what is natural of itself is void of life; and that the life which appears in it, is from the life of the spiritual man, thus that this is what is judged; and moreover that being "judged according to deeds," means that man's spiritual is judged, may be seen in the work on Heaven and Hell, in the article headed, That Man after Death is such as his Life in the World was.

To these things I will add a certain heavenly arcanum, which is indeed mentioned in the work on Heaven and Hell, but has not yet been described. Every one after death is bound to some society, even when first he comes into the spiritual world. But a spirit in his first state is ignorant of it, for he is then in his externals and not yet in his internals. When he is in this state, he goes hither and thither, wherever the desires of his mind impel him; but still actually, he is where his love is, that is, in a society where those are who are in a love like his own. When a spirit is in such a state he then appears in many other places, in all of them also present as it were with the body, but this is only an appearance. Wherefore as soon as he is led by the Lord into his own ruling love, he vanishes instantly from the eyes of others, and is among his own, in the society to which he was bound. This peculiarity exists in the spiritual world, and is wonderful to those who are ignorant of its cause. Hence now it is, that as soon as spirits are gathered together, and separated, they are also judged, and every one is presently in his own place, the good in heaven, and in a society there among their own, and the evil in hell, and in a society there among their own. From these things it is moreover evident, that the Last Judgment can exist nowhere but in the spiritual world, both because every one there is in the likeness of his own life, and because he is with those who are in similar life, and thus everyone is with his own. But it is otherwise in the natural world; the good and the evil can dwell together there, the one ignorant of what the other is, nor are they separated from each other according to the love of their life. Indeed it is impossible for any one in the natural body, to be either in heaven or in hell; wherefore in order that man may come into one or the other, it is necessary that he put off his natural body, and be judged the spiritual body. Hence it is, as was said above, that the spiritual man is judged, and not the natural.

VI. THE LAST JUDGMENT EXISTS, WHEN THE END OF THE CHURCH IS; AND THE END OF THE CHURCH IS, WHEN THERE IS NO FAITH, BECAUSE THERE IS NO CHARITY. There are many reasons why the Last Judgment exists when the end of the church is. The principal reason is, that then the equilibrium between heaven and hell begins to perish, and with the equilibrium man's freedom itself; and when man's freedom perishes, he can no longer be saved, for he cannot then be led to heaven in freedom, but from freedom is borne to hell; for no man can be reformed without freedom, and all man's freedom is from the equilibrium between heaven and hell. That it is so, may appear from two articles in the work on Heaven and Hell, where it treats, Of the Equilibrium between Heaven and Hell : and, That Man is in that Freedom by means of that Equilibrium between Heaven and Hell ; and further, that no man can be reformed except in freedom.

That the equilibrium between heaven and hell begins to perish at the end of the church, may appear from this, that heaven and hell are from the human race, as shown above in its own article, and that when few men come into heaven, and many into hell, evil on the one part increases over good on the other; for evil increases in proportion as hell increases, and all man's evil is from hell, and all his good is from heaven. Now since evil increases over good at the end of the church, all are then judged by the Lord, the evil are separated from the good, all things are reduced into order, and a new heaven is established, and also a new church upon earth, and thus the equilibrium is restored. It is this then which is called the Last Judgment, of which more will be said in the following articles.

It is known from the Word, that the end of the church is, when faith no longer exists within it, but it is not yet known, that there is no faith, if there is no charity; therefore something shall now be said upon this subject. It is predicted by the Lord that there is no faith at the end of the church: When the Son of Man comes shall He find faith on the earth (Luke 18:8); and also that there is no charity then: In the consummation of the age iniquity will be multiplied, the charity of many will grow cold, and this gospel will be preached in all the world, and then shall the end come (Matt. 24:12, 14). "The consummation of the age" is the last time of the church. The state of the church successively decreasing as to love and faith, is described by the Lord in this chapter, but it is described there by mere correspondences, and therefore the things therein predicted by the Lord cannot be understood, unless the spiritual sense corresponding to each expression there is known; on which account it has been granted me by the Lord to explain in the Arcana Coelestia the whole of that chapter and a part of the next, concerning the consummation of the age, His advent, the successive vastation of the church, and the Last Judgment; see in the Arcana Coelestia.

Something shall now be said concerning this, that there is no faith, if there is no charity. It is supposed that faith exists, so long as the doctrinals of the church are believed; or that they who believe, have faith; and yet mere believing is not faith, but willing and doing what is believed, is faith. When the doctrinals of the church are merely believed, they are not in man's life, but only in his memory, and thence in the thought of his external man; nor do they enter into his life, before they enter into his will, and thence into his actions: then for the first time does faith exist in man's spirit; for man's spirit, the life of which is his life itself, is formed from his will, and from so much of his thought as proceeds from his will; the memory of man, and the thought derived from it, being only the outer court by which introduction is effected. Whether you say the will, or the love, it is the same, since every one wills what he loves, and loves what he wills; and the will is the receptacle of love, and the intellect, the function of which is to think, is the receptacle of faith. A man may know, think, and understand many things, but those which do not accord with his will or love, he rejects from him when he is left to himself, to meditate from his own will or love, and therefore he also rejects them after the life of the body, when he lives in the spirit; for that alone remains in man's spirit which has entered into his will or love, as was said above. Other things after death are viewed as foreign, which he casts out of doors, and regards with aversion, because they are not of his love. But it is another thing when man not only believes the doctrinals of the church which are from the Word, but wills them, and does them; then he has faith; for faith is the affection of truth from willing truth because it is truth; for to will truth itself because it is truth is the spiritual man, for it is withdrawn from the natural, which consists in willing truth, not for truth's sake, but for the sake of self-glory, fame and gain. Truth regarded apart from such things is spiritual, because in its essence it is Divine; wherefore, to will truth because it is truth, is also to acknowledge, and to love the Divine. These two are altogether conjoined, and are also regarded as one in heaven, for the Divine which proceeds from the Lord in heaven is Divine truth, as may be seen in the work on Heaven and Hell, and they are angels in the heavens, who receive it, and make it of their life. These things are said, in order that it may be known, that faith is not only to believe, but to will and do, therefore there is no faith if there is no charity. Charity or love is to will and to do.

That within the church at this day, faith is so rare, that it can scarcely be said to exist at all, was made evident, from many both learned and simple, whose spirits were explored after death, as to what their faith had been in the world; and it was found, that every one of them supposed faith to be merely to believe, and to persuade himself that it is so; and that the more learned of them placed it entirely in believing, with trust or confidence that they are saved by the Lord's passion and His intercession, and that scarcely one among them knew that there is no faith, if there is no charity, or love yea, they did not know what charity to the neighbor is, nor the difference between thinking and willing. For the most part they turned their backs upon charity, saying that charity effects nothing, but faith only. When it was said to them, that charity and faith are one, like the will and the understanding, and that charity has its seat in the will, and faith in the understanding, and that to separate the one from the other, is like separating the will from the understanding, this they did not understand. Whence it was made evident to me that scarcely any faith exists at the present day. This also was shown them to the life. They who were in the persuasion that they had faith, were led to an angelic society, where genuine faith existed, and when they were made to communicate with it, they clearly perceived that they had no faith, which afterwards moreover, they confessed in the presence of many. The same thing was also shown by other means to those who had made a profession of faith, and had thought they believed, without having lived the life of faith, which is charity; and every one of them confessed that they had no faith, because they had nothing of it in the life of their spirits, but only in some thought extrinsic to it, whilst they lived in the natural world.

Such is the state of the church at this day, namely, that in it there is no faith because there is no charity; and where there is no charity, there is no spiritual good, for that good exists from charity alone. It was said from heaven that there is still good with some, but that it cannot be called spiritual, but natural good, because Divine truths themselves are in obscurity, and Divine truths introduce to charity, for they teach it, and regard it as their end and aim; whence no other charity can exist than such as the truths are which form it. The Divine truths from which the doctrines of the churches are derived, respect faith alone, on which account they are called the doctrines of faith, and do not look to life; and truths which only regard faith and not life, cannot make man spiritual; for so long as they are out of the life they are only natural, being merely known and thought of like other things. Hence it is that spiritual good is not given at the present day, but only natural good with some. Moreover every church in the beginning is spiritual, for it begins from charity; but in the course of time it turns aside from charity to faith, and then from being an internal church it becomes an external one, and when it becomes external its end is, since it then places everything in knowledge, and little or nothing in life. Thus also as far as man from being internal becomes external, spiritual light is darkened within him, until he no longer sees Divine truth from truth itself, that is from the light of heaven, for Divine truth is the light of heaven, but only from natural light; which is of such a nature, that when it is alone, and not illumined by spiritual light, it sees Divine truth as it were in night, and recognizes it as truth for no other reason than that it is so called by the leader, and is received as such by the common assembly. Hence it is, that their intellectual faculty cannot be illustrated by the Lord, for as far as natural light shines in the intellectual faculty, in so far spiritual light is obscured. Natural light shines in the intellectual faculty, when worldly, corporeal, and earthly things are loved in preference to spiritual, celestial, and Divine things; so far also man is external.

But since it is not known in the Christian world that there is no faith if there is no charity, nor what charity towards the neighbor is, nor even that the will constitutes the man himself, and the thought only in as far as it is derived from the will, therefore, in order that these subjects may come into the light of the understanding, I will adjoin a collection of passages concerning them from the Arcana Coelestia, which may serve for illustration. FROM THE ARCANA COELESTIA. FAITH. They who do not know that all things in the universe refer themselves to truth and good, and to the conjunction of both, in order to the production of anything, do not know that all things of the church refer themselves to faith and love, and to the conjunction of both. All things in the universe refer themselves to truth and good, and to their conjunction. Truths belong to faith, and goods to love. They who do not know that each and all things in man have relation to the understanding and the will, and to the conjunction of both, in order that man may be man, also do not know that all things of the church have relation to faith and love, and to their conjunction, in order that the church may be in man. Man has two faculties, one of which is called the understanding, and the other the will. The understanding is dedicated to the reception of truths, or of those things which belong to faith; and the will to the reception of goods, or of those things which belong to love. Hence it follows, that love or charity makes the church, and not faith alone, or faith separated from them. Faith separated from charity is no faith. Such faith perishes in the other life. Doctrinals concerning faith alone, destroy charity. They who separate faith from charity are represented in the Word by Cain, by Ham, by Reuben, by the firstborn of the Egyptians, and by the Philistines. As far as charity departs, in so far prevails a religion respecting faith alone. The church in process of time turns aside from charity to faith, and at length to faith alone. In the last time of the church there is no faith, because there is no charity. They who make faith alone saving, excuse a life of evil; and they who are in a life of evil, have no faith, because they have no charity. They are inwardly in the falsities of their own evil, although they do not know it. Therefore good cannot be conjoined to them. Also in the other life they are opposed to good, and to those who are in good. The simple in heart know better than the learned what the good of life is, and thus what charity is, but not what separated faith is. Good is the esse, and truth the existere derived from it, and thus the truth of faith has its own esse of life from the good of charity. Hence the truth of faith lives from the good of charity, or charity is the life of faith. Faith is not alive in man, when he only knows and thinks of the things of faith, but when he wills them, and from willing, does them. The conjunction of the Lord with man is not by faith, but by the life of faith, which is charity. Worship from the good of charity is true worship, but worship from the truth of faith, without the good of charity, is merely an external act. Faith alone, or faith separated from charity, is as the light of winter, in which all things of the earth are torpid, and nothing is produced; but faith with charity is as the light of spring and of summer, in which they all bloom and are made productive. The wintry light, which is that of separated faith, in the other life is turned into dense darkness, when the light of heaven inflows; and they who are in that faith, then come into blindness and stupidity. They who separate faith from charity, are in darkness, and thus in ignorance of truth, and thence in falsities, for falsities are darkness. They cast themselves into falsities, and hence into evils. The errors and falsities into which they cast themselves. The Word is closed against them. They do not see and attend to all the things which the Lord so often spoke concerning love and charity, which see. They neither know what good is, what heavenly love is, nor what charity is.

Charity makes the church, and not faith separated from charity. How much of good would exist in the church, if charity were regarded as primary. The church would he one, and not divided into many, if charity were its essential; and then it would be unimportant if men did differ on the doctrines of faith and of external worship. All in heaven are regarded from charity, and none from faith without it. The twelve disciples of the Lord represented the church, as to the all of faith and charity, in one complex, as in like manner did the twelve tribes of Israel. Peter, James and John, represented faith, charity, and the goods of charity, in their order. Peter represented faith and John the goods of charity (Pref. to chap. 18 and 22 of Genesis). In the last times, there would be no faith in the Lord, because no charity, was represented by Peter's denying the Lord three times, before the cock crew twice; for Peter there in a representative sense is faith. "Cockcrowing," as well as "twilight," signifies in the Word the last time of the church. And "three" or "thrice," signify what is complete to the end. The like is signified by what the Lord said to Peter, when Peter saw John following the Lord: What is it to thee, Peter? Follow thou Me, John; for Peter said of John: What is he (John 21:21, 22;)? John rested on the breast of the Lord, because he represented the goods or charity. All the names of persons and places in the Word signify things abstracted from them. CHARITY. That heaven is distinguished into two kingdoms, one of which is called the celestial kingdom, and the other the spiritual; love in the celestial kingdom is love to the Lord, and is called celestial love; and love in the spiritual kingdom is charity towards the neighbor, and is called spiritual love. Heaven is distinguished into those two kingdoms, may be seen in the work on Heaven and Hell. And the Divine of the Lord in the heavens is love to Him, and charity towards the neighbor , in the same work. It is not known what good and truth are, unless it he known what love to the Lord and charity towards the neighbor are, because all good is of love and charity, and all truth is of good. To know truths, to will truths, and to be affected by truths for truth's sake, that is, because they are truths, is charity. Charity consists in an internal affection of doing truth, and not in an external affection without it. Therefore charity consists in performing uses for the sake of uses, and its kind is according to the uses. Charity is man's spiritual life. The whole Word is the doctrine of love and charity. Men at this day do not know what charity is. Still it may be known from the light of reason, that love and charity constitute man. Also that good and truth agree together, and one belongs to the other; therefore charity and faith do the like. In the supreme sense the Lord is the neighbor, because He is to be loved above all things; hence all that is the neighbor which is from Him, and in which He is; therefore good and truth are the neighbor. The distinction of neighbor is according to the quality of good; thus according to the presence of the Lord. Every man, and every society, also our country, and the church, and in the universal sense the kingdom of the Lord, are the neighbor; and to do well by them, from the good of love, according to their several states, is to love the neighbor; thus the neighbor is their good, which we ought to consult. Civil good, which is justice, and moral good, which is the good of life in society, are also the neighbor. To love the neighbor is not to love the person, but that in him which makes him the neighbor, that is, good and truth. They who love the person, and not that which makes the neighbor in him, love the evil as well as the good. And they do service to the evil as well as to the good, when yet to serve the evil is to injure the good, and this is not to love the neighbor. The judge who punishes the evil to amend them, and lest they should corrupt the good, loves the neighbor. To love the neighbor is to do what is good, just, and upright in every work, and in every function. Hence charity towards the neighbor extends itself, both in general and in particular, to all that a man thinks, wills, and does. To do good and truth for the sake of good and truth, is to love the neighbor. They who do this, love the Lord, who in the supreme sense, is the neighbor. A life of charity is a life according to the Lord's precepts; so that to live according to Divine truths, is to love the Lord. Genuine charity is not meritorious. Because it is from an internal affection, thus from the delight of doing good. They who separate faith from charity, in the other life make a merit of faith, and of the good works they did, as matters of external form. The doctrine of the Ancient Church was the doctrine of life, which is the doctrine of charity. The ancients, who were of the church, arranged the goods of charity in order, and distinguished them into classes, giving names to each, and this was the source of their wisdom. Wisdom and intelligence increase immensely in the other life, with those who have lived a life of charity in the world. The Lord inflows with Divine truths into charity, because into the very life of man. Man is as a garden, when charity and faith are conjoined in him, but as a desert when they are not conjoined. Man recedes from wisdom in proportion as he recedes from charity. They who are not in charity, are in ignorance of Divine truths, howsoever wise they may think themselves. The angelic life consists in performing the goods of charity, which are uses. The spiritual angels are forms of charity. THE WILL AND THE UNDERSTANDING. Man has two faculties, one of which is called the understanding, and the other the will. Those two faculties make the man himself. The man is such, as those two faculties are in him. By them also man is distinguished from the beasts, because the understanding of man may be elevated by the Lord, and see Divine truths, and his will may be elevated equally, and perceive Divine goods; and thus man may be conjoined to the Lord by those two faculties, which make him man; but that it is not so with beasts. And since man, in that faculty, is above the beasts, he cannot die as to his interiors, which belong to his spirit, but he lives to eternity (n. 5302). All things in the universe refer themselves to good and truth; thus in man to the will and the understanding. For the understanding is the recipient of truth, and the will of good. It amounts to the same whether you say truth, or faith, for faith is of truth, and truth is of faith; and also whether you say good, or love, for love is of good, and good is of love; for what a man believes, he calls truth; and what he loves, he calls good. Hence it follows, that the understanding is the recipient of faith, and the will is the recipient of love. And since man's understanding may be receptive of faith towards God, and his will of love towards God, that he may be conjoined to God by faith and love, and whoso can be conjoined to God by faith and love, can never die. The will of man is the very esse of his life, since it is the receptacle of love or good, and the understanding is the existere of his life derived form it, since it is the receptacle of faith or truth. Thus the life of the will is the principle life of man, and the life of the understanding proceeds from it. Just as light proceeds form fire or flame. The things which enter the understanding and the will at the same time, are appropriated to man, but not those which enter the understanding alone. Those things become properties of man's life, which are received by the will. Hence if follows, that man is man from the will, and form the understanding thence. Every man moreover is loved and esteemed by others, according to the good of his will and the understanding thence; for he who wills well, and understands well, is loved and esteemed, but he who understands well, and does not will well, is rejected and despised. Man also after death remains as his will, and the understanding thence. And those things which belong to the understanding, and not at the same time to the will, then vanish away, because they are not in man. Or, what amounts to the same, man remains after death as his love, and its derivative faith are, or as his good and its derivative truth are; and the things which belong to faith, and not at the same time to love, or the things which belong to truth, and not at the same time to good, then vanish away, because they are not in man, and thus not of man. Man may receive in the understanding what he does not do from the will, or he may understand what he cannot will, because it is against his love. The reason why man scarcely knows the distinction between thinking and willing. How perverted is the state of those whose understanding and will do not act in unity. Such is the state of hypocrites, of deceivers, of flatterers, and of dissemblers. All the will of good, and all the derivative understanding of truth are from the Lord; not so the understanding of truth, separated from the will of good. It is the understanding which is enlightened by the Lord. The understanding is enlightened as far as man receives truth in the will, that is, as far as he wills to do according to it (n. 3619). The understanding has light from heaven, as the sight has light from the world. The understanding is such, as are the truths from good of which it is formed. The understanding is that which is from truths from good, but not that which is from falsities from evil. The understanding is the seeing, from matters of experience and science, truths, the causes of things, connections, and consequences, in series. The understanding is the seeing and perceiving whether a thing be truth, before it is confirmed, but not the being able to confirm every thing. The seeing and perceiving whether a thing be truth before it is confirmed, is given to those only who are affected with truth for the sake of truth, and are thus in spiritual light. The light of confirmation is natural light, communicable even to the evil. That all dogmas, even false ones, may be confirmed, until they appear like truths.

VII. ALL THE THINGS WHICH ARE PREDICTED IN THE APOCALYPSE, ARE AT THIS DAY FULFILLED. No one can know what all the things which are contained in the Apocalypse signify and involve, unless he knows the internal or spiritual sense of the Word; for everything there is written in a style similar to that of the prophecies of the Old Testament, in which each Word signifies some spiritual thing, which does not appear in the sense of the letter. Besides, the contents of the Apocalypse cannot be explained as to their spiritual sense, except by one who also knows how it went with the church, even to its end, which can only be known in heaven, and is the thing contained in the Apocalypse. For the spiritual sense of the Word treats everywhere of the spiritual world, that is, of the state of the church in the heavens, as well as in the earth; hence the Word is spiritual and Divine. It is this state which is there expounded in its own order. Hence it may appear, that the things contained in the Apocalypse can never be explained by any one but him to whom a revelation has been made concerning the successive states of the church in the heavens; for there is a church in the heavens as well as on the earth, of which something shall be said in the following articles.

The quality of the Lord's church on earth, cannot be seen by any man, so long as he lives in the world, still less how the church in process of time has turned aside from god to evil. The reason is, that man whilst he is living in the world, is in externals, and only sees those things which appear before his natural man; but the quality of the church as to spiritual things, which are its internals, does not appear in the world. Yet it does appear in heaven as in clear day, for the angels are in spiritual thought, and also in spiritual sight, and hence see nothing but spiritual things. Furthermore, all the men who have been born in this world from the beginning of creation are together in the spiritual world, as shown above, and are all there distinguished into societies according to the goods of love and faith, as may be seen in the work on Heaven and Hell; whence it is that the state of the church, and its progressions, are manifest in heaven before the angels. Now since the state of the church as to love and faith is described in the spiritual sense of the Apocalypse, therefore no one can know what all the things in its series involve, but he to whom it has been revealed from heaven, and to whom at the same time it has been granted to know the internal or spiritual sense of the Word. This I can assert, that each thing there, nay, that every word, contains within it a spiritual sense, and all things of the church, as to its spiritual state, from the beginning to the end, are fully described in that sense; and because every word there signifies some spiritual thing, therefore not a word can be wanting without the series of things in the internal sense thereby suffering a change; on which account, at the end of that book, it is said: If any one shall take away from the words of the book of this prophecy, God will take away his part out of the book of life, and from that holy city, and from those things which are written in that book (Apoc. 22:19). It is the same with the books of the Old Testament; in them also every thing, and every word, contains an internal or spiritual sense, wherefore not one word can be taken away from them either. Hence it is that, of the Lord's Divine providence, those books have been preserved entire to an iota since the time in which they were written, and by the care of many who have enumerated their minutest particulars; this was provided by the Lord on account of the sanctity which is within each iota, letter, word, and thing they contain.

Since in like manner there is an internal or spiritual sense in every word in the Apocalypse, and since that sense contains the arcana of the state of the church in the heavens, and on the earth; and since those arcana can be revealed to no one, but to him who knows that sense, and to whom at the same time it has been granted to have consort with the angels, and to speak spiritually with them, therefore, lest the things which are therein written should be hidden to men, and should hereafter be disregarded, because they are not understood, its contents have been disclosed to me; but because they are many they cannot be described in this little work. On which account I will explain the whole book from beginning to end, and disclose the arcana which are within it. This explanation shall be published in less than two years, together with certain things in Daniel, which have hitherto lain hidden, because their spiritual sense was unknown.

He who does not know the internal or spiritual sense, never can divine what is meant in the Apocalypse by "the dragon," and by "the battle" of Michael and his angels with it; what by "the tail" with which the dragon drew down the third part of the stars from heaven; what by "the woman" who brought forth the son a male, which was caught up to God, and whom the dragon persecuted; what by "the beast ascending from the sea," and "the beast ascending from the earth," which had so many horns; what by "the harlot," with whom the kings of the earth committed whoredom;

what by the first and second "resurrection," and by "the thousand years"; what by "the lake of sulphur and of fire," into which the dragon, the beast, and the false prophet were cast; what by "the white horse"; also what by "the former heaven, and the former earth" which passed away; and what by "the new heaven and the new earth," in the place of the former; and by "the sea," which was no more; also what by "the city New Jerusalem descending from heaven," and by its "measures," "wall," "gates," and "foundation of precious stones"; what by the various "numbers"; besides other things, which are the deepest mysteries to those who know nothing of the spiritual sense of the Word. But the meaning of all these things shall be unfolded in the promised explanation of that book.

It has been remarked before, that all the things which are contained in that book, in the heavenly sense, are now fulfilled. In this little work I will deliver some general account of the Last Judgment, the Babylon destroyed, the first heaven and the first earth which passed away, the new heaven, the new earth, and the New Jerusalem; in order that it may be known, that all things are now accomplished. But the details can only be delivered, where all these things are explained according to the description of them in the Book of Revelation

VIII. THE LAST JUDGMENT HAS BEEN ACCOMPLISHED. It was shown above, in an article for the purpose, that the Last Judgment does not exist on the earth, but in the spiritual world, where all from the beginning of creation are together; and since it is so, it is impossible for any man to know when the Last Judgment is accomplished, for every one expects it to exist on earth, accompanied by a change of all things in the visible heaven, and on the earth and in the human race there. Lest therefore the man of the church from ignorance should live in such a belief, and lest they who think of the Last Judgment should expect it forever, whence at length the belief in those things which are said of it in the literal sense of the Word must perish, and lest perchance therefore many should recede from a belief in the Word, it has been granted me to see with my own eyes that the Last Judgment is now accomplished; that the evil are cast into the hells, and the good elevated into heaven, and thus that all things are reduced into order, the spiritual equilibrium between good and evil, or between heaven and hell, being thence restored. It was granted me to see from beginning to end how the Last Judgment was accomplished; and also how Babylon was destroyed, also how those who are meant by "the dragon" were cast into the abyss, and how the New Heaven was formed, and the New Church instituted in the heavens, which is meant by "the New Jerusalem." It was granted me to see all these things with my own eyes, in order that I might be able to testify of them. This Last Judgment was commenced in the beginning of the year 1757, and was fully accomplished at the end of that year.

But it is to be known that the Last Judgment was effected upon those who had lived from the Lord's time to this day, but not upon those who had lived before. For a Last Judgment had twice before existed on this earth; one which is described in the Word by "the flood," the other was effected by the Lord Himself when He was in the world, which is also meant by the Lord's words: Now is the judgment of this world, now is the prince of this world cast out (John 12:31); and in another place: These things I have spoken unto you that in Me ye may have peace; be of good cheer, I have overcome the world (John 16:33); and also by these words in Isaiah: Who is this that cometh from Edom, walking in the multitude of His strength, great to save? I have trodden the wine-press alone, therefore I have trodden them in My anger; whence their victory is sprinkled upon My garments, for the day of vengeance is in My heart, and the year of My redeemed has come; therefore He became a Savior (Isa. 63:1-8); and in many other places. A Last Judgment has twice before existed on this earth, because every judgment exists at the end of a church, as shown above in an article for the purpose, and there have been two churches on this earth, one before the flood, and one after it. The church before the flood is described in the first chapters of Genesis by the new creation of the heaven and the earth, and by paradise; its end, by the eating of the tree of science, and the subsequent particulars; and its Last Judgment by the flood; the whole by mere correspondences, according to the style of the Word; in the internal or spiritual sense of which, by "the creation of the heaven and the earth," the institution of a new church is meant, see the first article; by "the paradise in Eden," its celestial wisdom; by "the tree of science," and by "the serpent," the scientific which destroyed it; and by "the flood," the Last Judgment upon the men of whom it consisted. But the other church, which was after the flood, is also described in certain passages in the Word (as in Deut. 32:7-14), and elsewhere. This church was extended through much of the Asiatic world, and was continued with the posterity of Jacob. Its end was, when the Lord came into the world. A Last Judgment was then effected by Him upon all who belonged to that church from its first institution; and, at the same time, upon the residue from the first church, The Lord came into the world for that end, to reduce all things in the heavens into order, and through the heavens all things on earth, and at the same time to make His Human Divine; for if this had not been done, no one could have been saved. That there were two churches on this earth before the Lord's coming is shown in various passages in the Arcana Coelestia, a collection of which may be seen below; and that the Lord came into the world to reduce all things in the heavens into order, and through them all things on earth, and to make His Human Divine. The third church on this earth is the Christian. Upon this church, and, at the same time, upon all those who had been in the first heaven since the Lord's time, the Last Judgment of which I now treat, was effected. The first and Most Ancient Church on this earth was that which is described in the first chapters of Genesis, and it was a celestial church, the chief of all the churches. Their quality they who were of that church are in heaven. They are in the greatest light there. There were various churches after the flood, which are called in one word, the Ancient Church. Through what kingdoms of Asia the Ancient Church was extended. The quality of the men of the Ancient Church. The Ancient Church was a representative church. What the quality of the Ancient Church was, when it began to decline. The distinction between the Most Ancient and Ancient Church. Of the church that commenced from Eber, which was called the Hebrew church. The distinction between the Ancient and the Hebrew church. Of the church instituted among the posterity of Jacob, or sons of Israel. The statutes, judgments and laws, which were commanded among the sons of Israel, were in part like those which existed in the Ancient Church. In what manner the representative rites of the church which was instituted among the sons of Israel, differed from the representative rites of the Ancient Church. In the Most Ancient Church there was immediate revelation from heaven; in the Ancient Church revelation by correspondences; in the church among the sons of Israel, by a living voice; and in the Christian church by the Word. The Lord was the God of the Most Ancient

Church, and also of the Ancient Church, and was called Jehovah. The Lord, when He was in the world, reduced all things in the heavens and in the hells into order. The Lord then freed the spiritual world from the antediluvian. Their quality. The Lord by temptations and victories subjugated the hells, and reduced all things into order, and at the same time glorified His Human. The Lord effected this by Himself, or by His own Power. The Lord alone fought. Hence the Lord alone became righteousness and merit. Thus the Lord united His Human with the Divine. The passion of the cross was the last temptation, and plenary victory, by which He glorified Himself, that is, made His Human Divine, and subjugated the hells. The Lord could not be tempted as to the Divine Itself. Therefore He assumed a human from the mother, into which He admitted temptations. He expelled whatever was hereditary from the mother, and put off the human He received from her, even until He was her son no longer, and He put on the Human Divine. The Lord saved men by the subjugation of the hells, and the glorification of His Human.

How this Last Judgment was effected cannot be described in all its details in this little work, for they are many, but shall be described in the Explanation of the Apocalypse. For the judgment was accomplished not only upon all the men of the Christian church, but also upon all who are called Mohammedans, and, moreover, upon all the Gentiles in the whole world. And it was effected in this order: first upon those of the Papal religion; then upon the Mohammedans; afterwards upon the Gentiles; and lastly upon the Reformed. The judgment upon those who were of the Papal religion shall be shown in the following article, on Babylon which has been destroyed; the judgment upon the Reformed in the article, on the first heaven which passed away; but something shall be said in this article, on the judgment upon the Mohammedans and Gentiles.

The following was seen to be the arrangement in the spiritual world of all the nations and people to be judged Collected in the middle, appeared those who are called the Reformed, where they were also distinct according to their countries; the Germans there towards the north; the Swedes there towards the west; the Danes in the west; the Dutch towards the east and the south; the English in the center. Surrounding this whole mid-region in which were the Reformed, appeared collected those of the Papal religion, the greater part of them in the western, some part in the southern quarter. Beyond them were the Mohammedans, also distinct according to their countries, who all appeared in the south-west. Beyond these, the Gentiles were congregated in vast numbers, constituting the very circumference. Beyond these appeared as it were a sea, which was the boundary. This arrangement of the nations in the various quarters, was an arrangement according to each nation's common faculty of receiving Divine truths; for in the spiritual world every one is known from the quarter, and the part of it, in which he dwells; and, moreover, in a society with many, he is known from his tarryings with reference to the quarters; concerning which, see the work on Heaven and Hell. It is the same when he goes from place to place; all advance to the quarters is then effected according to the successive states of the thoughts from the affections which belong to his own life; in accordance with which all those who are spoken of in what follows were led to their own places. In a word, the ways in which every one walks in the spiritual world are actual determinations of the thoughts of the mind; whence it is, that "ways," "walking," and the like, in the spiritual sense of the Word, signify the determinations and progressions of spiritual life.

In the Word, the four quarters are called "the four winds," and a gathering is called "a gathering from the four winds"; as where the Last Judgment is the subject treated of in Matthew: He shall send His angels, and they shall gather together the elect from the four winds, from one end of the heavens to the other ; and elsewhere: All nations shall be gathered together before the Son of man, and He shall separate them one from another, as a shepherd separates the sheep from the goats, and He shall set the sheep on the right and the goats on the left (Matt. 25:31, 32). This signifies that the Lord will then separate those who are in truths and at the same time in good, from those who are in truths and not in good; for in the spiritual sense of the Word, "the right" signifies good, and "the left" truth, and "sheep" and "goats" the same. The judgment was effected upon these alone; the evil who were in no truths being in the hells already; for all the evil in heart who have denied the Divine, and have rejected the truths of the church from their belief are cast thither alter death, and therefore before the judgment. "The first heaven" which passed away, consisted of those who were in truths, and not in good, and "the new heaven" was formed of those who were in truths, and at the same time in good.

As regards the judgment upon the Mohammedans and Gentiles, which is treated of in this article, it was thus effected. The Mohammedans were led forth from their places, where they were gathered together in the south-west, by a way round the Christians, from the west, through the north, to the east, as far as its southern boundary; and the good were separated from the evil in the way. The evil were cast into marshes and lakes, many too being scattered about in a certain far desert. But the good were led through the east to a land of great extent near the south, and habitations were there given them. They who were led thither had in the world acknowledged the Lord as the greatest Prophet, and as the Son of God, and had believed that He was sent by the Father to instruct the human race, and at the same time had lived a moral spiritual life according to their religious principles. Most of these, when instructed, receive faith in the Lord, and acknowledge Him to be one with the Father. Communication is also granted them with the Christian heaven, by influx from the Lord; but they are not commingled with it, because religion separates them. All of that religion, as soon as they come into the other life among their own, first seek Mohammed, yet he does not appear, but in his place there are two others, who call themselves Mohammeds, and who have obtained seats in the middle, under the Christian heaven, towards the left part of it. These two are in the place of Mohammed, because all after death, what ever be their religion, are first led to those they had worshiped in the world, for every one's religion adheres to him, but they recede on perceiving that these can render them no assistance. They are thus yielded up into their own religion at first, as the only possible means of effecting their withdrawal from it. Where Mohammed himself is, and what he is, and whence come those two who fill his place, shall be told in the book in which the Apocalypse is explained.

The judgment was effected upon the Gentiles in nearly the same manner as upon the Mohammedans; but they were not led like them in a circuit, but only a short way in the west, where the evil were separated from the good, the evil being there cast into two great gulfs, which stretched obliquely into the deep, but the good were conducted above the middle, where the Christians were, towards the land of the Mohammedans in the eastern quarter, and dwellings were given them behind, and beyond the

Mohammedans, to a great extent in the southern quarter. But those of the Gentiles who in the world had worshiped God under the Human form, and bad led lives of charity according to their religious principles, were conjoined with Christians in heaven, for they acknowledge and adore the Lord more than others; the most intelligent of them are from Africa The multitude of the Gentiles and Mohammedans who appeared, was so great, that it could be numbered only by myriads. The judgment on this vast multitude was effected in a few days, for every one after being yielded up into his own love and into his own faith, is immediately assigned and carried to his like.

From all these particulars appears the truth of the Lord's prediction concerning the Last Judgment, that: They shall come from the east and west, and from the north and south, and shall sit down in the kingdom of God (Luke 13:29).

IX. BABYLON AND ITS DESTRUCTION. That all the things which are predicted in the Apocalypse are at this day fulfilled, may be seen above ; and that the Last Judgment has already been accomplished, may be seen in the preceding article; where it is also shown how the judgment was effected upon the Mohammedans and Gentiles. Now follows an account of the manner in which it was effected upon the Papists, who are meant by "Babylon," which is treated of in many parts of the Apocalypse, and its destruction especially in chapter 18, where it is thus described: An angel cried vehemently with a great voice, Babylon hath fallen, hath fallen, and has become the habitation of demons, and the hold of every foul spirit, and the cage of every unclean and hateful bird. But before it is told how that destruction was effected, I shall premise: I. What is meant by "Babylon," and what its quality is. II. The quality of those in the other life who are of Babylon. III. Where their habitations have hitherto been. IV. Why they were there tolerated until the day of the Last Judgment. V. How they were destroyed, and their habitations made a desert. VI. Those of them who were in the affection of truth from good were preserved. VII. The state of those hereafter who come thence from the earth.

I. What is meant by Babylon, and what its quality is. By Babylon are meant all who wish to have dominion by religion. To have dominion by religion, is to have dominion over men's souls, thus over their very spiritual life, and to use the Divine things, which are in their religion, as the means. All those who have dominion for an end, and religion for the means are in general Babylon. They are called Babylon because such dominion began in ancient times; but it was destroyed in its beginning. Its commencement is described by the city and the tower, the head of which was to be in heaven; and its destruction, by the confusion of lips, whence its name Babel was derived (Gen. 11:1-9). What the particulars there related mean in the internal or spiritual sense of the Word, may be seen explained in the Arcana Coelestia. Moreover that this dominion began and was instituted in Babel, appears in Daniel, where it is said of Nebuchadnezzar, that he set up an image which all were to adore. And it is also meant by Belshazzar and his peers drinking out of the golden and silver vessels, which Nebuchadnezzar had carried away from the temple of Jerusalem, at the same time they worshiped gods of gold, silver, copper, and iron; wherefore it was written on the wall: He hath numbered, he hath weighed, he hath divided; and on the same night the king himself was slain. "The vessels of gold and silver" of the temple of Jerusalem, signify the goods and truths of the church; "drinking out of them," and at the same time worshiping gods of gold, silver, copper, and iron, signify profanation; and "the writing upon the wall," and "the death of the king" signify visitation, and destruction denounced against those who make use of Divine goods and truths as means. What their quality is who are called Babylon, is also described sometimes in the prophets; as in Isaiah: Thou mayest take up this parable concerning the king of Babylonia. Jehovah hath broken the staff of the wicked, the scepter of those having dominion; thou, Lucifer, hast fallen from heaven; thou art cut down even to the earth; thou hast said in thy mind, I will ascend into the heavens; I will exalt my throne over the stars of God, and I sit on the mountain of the assembly, in the sides of the north, I will become like the Most High. Nevertheless thou shalt be cast down into hell, to the sides of the pit; I will cut off the name and residue of Babylon and will cause her to become an hereditary possession of the bittern (14:4, 5, 12, 13, 14, 15, 22, 23). And again it is said in the same: The lion said, Babylon is fallen, is fallen, and all the graven images of her god are cast down. See also (47 and 48 14-20; and Jer. 50:1-3). From these passages it is now evident what Babylonia is. It should be known that the church becomes Babylonia, when charity and faith cease, and the love of self begins to rule in their place; for this love in proportion as it is unchecked, rushes on, aiming to dominate not merely over all whom it can subject to itself on earth, but even over heaven; nor does it rest there, but it climbs the very throne of God, and transfers to itself His Divine power. That it did this, even before the Lord's coming, appears from the passages of the Word adduced above. But that Babylonia was destroyed by the Lord when He was in the world, both by their becoming altogether idolatrous, and by the Last Judgment upon them in the spiritual world. This is meant by the prophetic sayings, that "Lucifer," who there is Babylon, was cast into hell, and that "Babylon has fallen"; and moreover by "the writing on the wall," and "the death of Belshazzar"; and also by "the stone, hewn from the rock," which destroyed the statue, of which Nebuchadnezzar dreamed.

But Babylon treated of in the Apocalypse, is the Babylon of this day, which arose after the Lord's coming, and is known to be with the Papists. This Babylon is more pernicious and more heinous than that which existed before the Lord's coming, because it profanes the interior goods and truths of the church, which the Lord revealed to the world, when He revealed Himself. How pernicious, how inwardly heinous it is: may appear from the following summary. They acknowledge and adore the Lord apart from all power of saving: they entirely separate His Divine from His Human, and transfer to themselves His Divine power, which belonged to His Human; for they remit sins; they send to heaven; they cast into hell; they save whom they will; they sell salvation; thus they arrogate to themselves what belongs to the Divine power alone: and since they exercise this power, it follows that thee make gods of themselves, each one according to his station, by transference from the highest of them, whom they call Christ's vicar, down to the lowest; thus they regard themselves as the Lord, and adore Him, not for His own sake, but for theirs. They not only adulterate and falsify the Word, but even take it away from the people, lest they should enter into the smallest light of truth; and not satisfied with this, they moreover annihilate it, acknowledging the Divine in the decrees of Rome, superior to the Divine in the Word; so that they exclude all from the way to heaven; for the acknowledgment of the Lord, faith in Him, and love to Him, are the way to heaven; and the Word is what teaches the way: whence it is, that without the Lord, by means of the Word, there is no salvation. They strive with all diligence to extinguish the light of heaven, which is from Divine truth, in order that ignorance may exist in the place of it, and the denser the ignorance, the more acceptable it is to them. They extinguish the light of heaven, by prohibiting the reading of the Word, and of books which contain doctrines from the Word; instituting worship by masses in a language not understood by the simple, and in which there is no Divine truth; and besides, they fill their world with falsities which are darkness itself, and which remove and dissipate the light. They likewise persuade the common people, that they have life in the faith of their priests, thus in the faith of another and not in their own. They also place all worship in a holy external, without the internal, making the internal empty, because it is without the knowledges of good and truth; and yet Divine worship is external, only so far as it is internal, since the external proceeds from the internal. Besides this, they introduce idolatries of various kinds, They make and multiply saints; they see and tolerate the adoration of these saints, and even the prayers offered to them almost as to gods; they set up their idols everywhere; boast of the great abundance of miracles done by them; set them over cities, temples, and monasteries; their bones taken out of their tombs they account holy, which yet are most vile; thus turning the minds of all from the worship of God, to the worship of men, Moreover, they use much artful precaution lest any one should come out of that thick darkness into light, from idolatrous worship to Divine worship; for they multiply monasteries, from which they send out spies and guards in all directions; they extort the confessions of the heart, which are also confessions of the thoughts and intentions, and if any one will not confess, they threaten him with infernal fire and torments in purgatory; and those who dare to speak against the Papal throne, and their dominion, they shut up in a horrible prison, which is called the inquisition. All these things they do for the sole end that they may possess the world and its treasures, and live in luxury and be the greatest, while the rest are slaves. But domination such as this, is not that of heaven over hell, but of hell over heaven, for as far as the love of having dominion is with man, especially with the man of the church, so far hell reigns. That this love reigns in hell, and makes hell, may be seen in the work on Heaven and Hell. From this summary it may appear that they have no church there, but Babylon; for the church is where the Lord Himself is worshiped, and where the Word is read. The attribution by the church, of two natures to the Lord, and thus the separation of His Divine from His Human, was effected in a council, for the sake of the Pope, that the Pope might he acknowledged as the Lord's vicar, disclosed from heaven in the Arcana Coelestia.

II. The quality of those in the other life who are Babylon can appear only to one to whom it has been given by the Lord to be together with those who are in the spiritual world. Since this has been granted to me, I am able to speak from experience, for I have seen them, I have heard them, and I have spoken with them. Every man after death is in a life similar to his life in the world; this cannot be changed, save only as regards the delights of the love, which are turned into correspondences, as may appear from the two articles in the work on Heaven and Hell. It is the same with the life of those now treated of, which is altogether such as it was in the world, with this difference, that the hidden things of their hearts are there uncovered, for they are in the spirit, in which reside the interior things of the thoughts and intentions, which they had concealed in the world, and had covered over with a holy external. And since these hidden things were then laid open, it was perceived that more than half of those who had usurped the power of opening and shutting heaven, were altogether atheists; but since dominion resides in their minds as in the world, and is based on this principle that all power was given by the Father to the Lord Himself, and that it was transferred to Peter, and by order of succession to the primates of the church, therefore an oral confession about the Lord remains adjoined to their atheism; but even this remains only so long as they enjoy some dominion by means of it. But the rest of them, who are not atheists, are so empty, as to be entirely ignorant of man's spiritual life, of the means of salvation, of the Divine truths which lead to heaven; and they know nothing at all of heavenly faith and love, believing that heaven may be granted of the Pope's favor to any one, whatever he be. Now since every one is in a life in the spiritual world, similar to his life in the natural world, without any difference, so long as he is neither in heaven nor in hell (as is shown, and may be seen in the work on Heaven and Hell,), and since the spiritual world, as regards its external appearance, is altogether like the natural world , therefore they also live a similar moral and civil life, and above all have similar worship, for this is inrooted, and inheres to man in his inmost, nor can any one after death be withdrawn from it, except he be in good from truths, and in truths from good. But it is more difficult to withdraw the nation now treated of from its worship, than other nations, because it is not in good from truths, and still less in truths from good; for its truths are not from the Word, with the exception of some few, which they have falsified by applying them to dominion; and hence it has none other than spurious good, for such as the truths are, such does the good become. These things are said, in order that it may be known, that the worship of this nation, in the spiritual world, is altogether similar to its worship in the natural world. These things premised, I will now relate some particulars of the worship and life of the Papists in the spiritual world. They have a certain council, in place of the council or consistory at Rome, in which their primates meet, and consult on various matters of their religion, especially on the means of holding the common people in blind obedience, and of enlarging their dominion. This council is situated in the southern quarter, near the east; but no one who has been a Pope or a cardinal in the world dares to enter it, because the semblance of Divine authority possesses their minds, from their having in the world arrogated the Lord's power to themselves; wherefore, as soon as they present themselves there, they are carried out, and cast to their like in a desert. But those among them, who have been upright in mind, and have not from confirmed belief usurped such power, are in a certain obscure chamber behind this council. There is another assembly in the western quarter, near the north; the business there, is the intromission of the credulous common people into heaven. They there dispose around them a number of societies which live in various external delights; in some of the societies they play, in some they dance, in some they compose the face into the various expressions of hilarity and mirthfulness; in some they converse in a friendly manner; in some they discuss civil affairs, in others religious matters; in other societies again, they talk obscenities; and so on, They admit their dependents into one of these societies such as each may desire, and call it heaven; but all of them, after being there a few hours, are wearied and depart, because those joys are external, and not eternal. In this way, moreover, many are withdrawn from a belief in their doctrinal concerning intromission into heaven. As regards their worship in particular, it is almost like their worship in the world; as in the world, it consists in masses, not performed in the common language of spirits, but in one composed of lofty-sounding words, which induce an external holiness and awe, and are utterly unintelligible. In like manner they adore saints, and expose idols to view; but their saints are nowhere to be seen, for all those who have sought to be worshiped as deities, are in hell; the rest who did not seek to be worshiped, are among common spirits. This their prelates know, for they seek and find them, and when found they despise them; yet they conceal it from the people, that the saints may still be worshiped as tutelar deities, but that the primates themselves, who are set over the people, may be worshiped as the lords of heaven. In like manner, moreover, they multiply temples and monasteries as they did in the world; they scrape together riches, and accumulate costly things, which they hide in cellars; for costly things exist in the spiritual, as well as in the natural world, and far more abundantly. In like manner they send forth monks, to allure the Gentiles to their religious persuasion, in order that they may subject them to their rule. They commonly have watch towers erected in the middle of their assemblies, from which they are enabled to enjoy an extended view into all the surrounding region. And moreover, by various means and arts they establish for themselves communications with persons far and near, joining in league with them, and drawing them over to their own party. Such is their state in general; but as to particulars, many prelates of that religion take away all power from the Lord, and claim it for themselves, and because they do this, they do not acknowledge any Divine. They still counterfeit holiness in externals; yet this holiness in itself is profane, because in their internals there is no acknowledgment of the Divine. Hence it is that they communicate with certain societies of the lowest heaven by a holy external, and with the hells by a profane internal, so that they are in both; on which account, moreover, they allure simple good spirits, and give them habitations near themselves, and also congregate wicked spirits, and dispose them around the society in all directions, by the simple good conjoining themselves with heaven, and by the wicked with hell. Hence they are enabled to accomplish heinous things which they perpetrate from hell. For the simple good who are in the lowest heavens look only to their holy external, and their very holy adoration of the Lord in externals, but they do not see their wickedness, and therefore they favor them, and this is their greatest protection; yet in process of time they all recede from their holy external, and then, being separated from heaven, they are cast into hell. From these things it may be known in some degree, what is the quality of those in the other life who are from Babylon. But I am aware that they who are in this world, and have no idea of man's state after death, of heaven, or of hell, but an inane and empty one, will wonder at the existence of such things in the spiritual world. But, that man is equally a man after death, that he lives in fellowships as he did in the world, that he dwells in houses, hears preaching in temples, discharges duties, and sees things in that world, similar to those in the former world he has left, may appear from all that has been said and shown of the things I have heard and seen, in the work on Heaven and Hell.

I have spoken with some from that nation, concerning the keys given to Peter; whether they believe that the power of the Lord over heaven and earth was transferred to him, and because this was the fundamental of their religion, they vehemently insisted on it, saying, that there was no doubt about it, because it was said manifestly. But when I asked them whether they knew that in each expression of the Word there is a spiritual sense, which is the sense of the Word in heaven, they said at first, that they did not know it, but afterwards they said they would inquire; and on inquiring, they were instructed that there is a spiritual sense within each expression of the Word, which differs from the sense of the letter, as the spiritual differs from the natural; and they were also instructed that no person named in the Word is named in heaven, but that some spiritual thing is there understood in place of him. Finally, they were informed, that instead of "Peter" in the Word is meant the truth of the faith of the church, from the good of charity, and that the same is meant by "a rock," which is there named with Peter, for it is said: Thou art Peter, and upon this rock will I build My church (Matt. 16:18, seq.). By this is not meant that any power was given to Peter, but that it is given to truth from good, for in the heavens all power belongs to truth from good, or to good through truth; and since all good, and all truth, are from the Lord, and nothing from man, that all power is the Lord's. When they heard this they replied indignantly, that they wished to know whether there is a spiritual sense in those words, wherefore the Word which is in heaven was given them, in which Word there is not the natural sense, but the spiritual, because it is for the angels, who are spiritual; that there is such a Word in heaven, may be seen in the work on Heaven and Hell. And when they read it, they saw manifestly that Peter is not named there, but truth from good, which is from the Lord, instead of him. Seeing this they rejected it with anger, and would almost have torn it in pieces with their teeth, had it not at that moment been taken away. Hence they were convinced, although unwilling to be convinced, that the Lord alone has that power, and by no means can it belong to any man, because it is the Divine power. The twelve disciples of the Lord represented the church as to the all of truth and good, or of faith and love, as in like manner did the twelve tribes of Israel. Peter, James, and John, represented faith, charity, and the goods of charity. Peter represented faith. The keys of the kingdom of heaven being given to Peter, signifies that all power is given to truth from good, or to faith from charity, proceeding from the Lord; thus that all power belongs to the Lord. "A key" signifies the power of opening and shutting. All power is in good by truths, or in truths from good, proceeding from the Lord. "A rock" in the Word signifies the Lord as to Divine truth. All names of persons and places in the Word signify things and states. Their names do not enter heaven, but are turned into the things they signify, and they cannot be pronounced in heaven. How elegant is the internal sense of the word, where mere names occur, is illustrated by examples.

III. Where their habitations in the spiritual world have hitherto been. It was said above), that all the nations and peoples in the spiritual world were seen to be as follows: collected in the middle appeared those who are called the Reformed; around this middle, those of the Papal religion; the Mohammedans, beyond them; and lastly the various Gentiles. Hence it may appear that the Papists formed the nearest circumference around the Reformed in the center. The reason of this is that they who are in the light of truth from the Word are in the center, and they who are in the light of truth from the Word are also in the light of heaven, for the light of heaven is from the Divine truth, and the Word is that in which this is. That the light of heaven is from the Divine truth, may be seen in the work on Heaven and Hell ; and that it is the Divine truth , Light, moreover, proceeds from the center towards the circumferences, and illuminates. Hence it is that the Papists proximately surround the center, for they have the Word, and it is also read by those of the ecclesiastical order, though not by the people. This is the reason why the Papal nation in the spiritual world have obtained habitations around those who are in the light of truth from the Word. Their manner of dwelling, before their habitations were utterly destroyed, and made into a desert, shall now be told. The greatest part of them dwelt in the south and in the west; but some in the north and in the east. In the south dwelt those who had excelled others in talent in the world, and had confirmed themselves in their own religion. Great numbers of the nobility and the rich also dwelt there. They did not dwell upon the earth there, but under it, from dread of robbers, guards being placed at the entrances. In that quarter, moreover, there was a great city, extending nearly from east to west, and somewhat into the west, situated very near the center where the Reformed were. Myriads of men or spirits tarried in that city. It was full of temples and monasteries. The ecclesiastics also carried into it all precious things which they were enabled by their various artifices to scrape together, and they hid them in its cells and subterranean crypts, which were so elaborately formed, that no one besides themselves could enter, for they were disposed around in the form of a labyrinth. On the treasures there amassed, in the full confidence that they could never be destroyed, they had set their hearts. When I saw those crypts I was amazed at the art displayed in constructing them, and enlarging them without end. The most of those who call themselves of the society of Jesus were there, and cultivated amicable relations with the rich who dwelt round about. Towards the east in that quarter was the council where they consulted on the enlargement of their dominion, and on the means of keeping the people in blind obedience. This concerning their habitations in the southern quarter. In the north, dwelt those who less excelled in ability, and had less confirmed themselves in their own religion, because they were in an obscure faculty of discerning and thence in blind faith. The multitude was not so great there as in the south. Most of them were in a great city extending lengthwise from the angle of the east to the west, and also a little into the west. It also was full of temples and monasteries. On its outmost side which was near the east there were many of various religions, and also some of the Reformed. A few places, moreover, beyond the city in that quarter, were occupied by the Papists. In the east dwelt those who had been in the greatest delight of ruling in the world, and at the same time in somewhat of natural light. They appeared there on mountains, but only in the quarter which faces the north; there were none in the other part which faces the south. In the angle towards the north, there was a mountain, on the top of which they had placed a certain one of unsound mind, whom, by communications of the thoughts, which are known in the spiritual, but unknown in the natural world, they were enabled to inspire to command anything they chose. And they gave out that he was the very God of heaven, appearing under a human form, and thus paid him Divine worship. They did this, because the people were desirous of receding from their idolatrous worship, wherefore, they devised it as a means of keeping them in obedience. That mountain is meant in Isaiah by "the mountain of assembly in the sides of the north," and those on the mountains are there meant by "Lucifer" (ver. 12); for such of the Babylonish crew as dwelt in the east, were in greater light than others, which light also, they had prepared for themselves by artifice. There also appeared some who were building a tower: which should reach even to heaven where the angels are, but this was only representative of their machinations; for machinations are presented in the spiritual world, before the eyes of those who stand at a distance, by many things which yet do not exist actually with those who are in the machinations: this is a common thing there. By this appearance it was given me to know what was signified by: The tower whose head should be in heaven, whence the place was called Babel (Gen. 11:1-10). These things are concerning their habitations in the east. In the west, in front, dwelt those of that religion who lived in the dark ages, for the most part underground, one posterity beneath another. The whole tract in front which looked to the north, was, as it were, excavated, and filled with monasteries. The entrances to them lay through caverns covered by roofs, through which they went out and in, They rarely spoke with those who lived in the following ages, being of a different disposition, and not so malicious; for as, in their times, there was no contention with the Reformed, there was there fore less of the craft and malice from hatred and revenge. In the western quarter beyond that tract, were many mountains, on which dwelt the wickedest of that nation, who in heart denied the Divine and yet orally professed their belief in Him, and adored Him with gestures more devoutly than others. They who were there, devised nefarious arts to keep the common people under the yoke of their sway, and also to force others to submit to that yoke: these arts it is not allowed to describe, they are so heinous. In general they are such as are mentioned in the work on Heaven and Hell, The mountains on which they dwelt, are meant in the Apocalypse by "the seven mountains," and those who were there are described by the woman sitting upon the scarlet beast: I saw a woman sitting upon a scarlet beast, full of names of blasphemy, having seven heads, and ten horns: she had on the forehead a name written, mystery, Babylon the great, mother of the whoredoms and abominations of the earth: the seven heads are seven mountains, on which the woman sitteth (Apoc. 17:3, 5, 9). By "a woman" in the internal sense, is meant the church, here in the opposite sense, a profane religion; by "the scarlet beast," the profanation of celestial love; by "the seven mountains," the profane lobe of ruling. These are concerning their habitations in the west. The reason why they dwell distinct according to quarters is, because all in the spiritual world are carried into that quarter, and into that part of it, which corresponds to their affections and loves, and no one to any other place; concerning which see the work on Heaven and Hell, where it treats of the four quarters of heaven. In general, all the consultations of the Babylonish race tend to this, that they may dominate, not only over heaven, but over the whole earth, and thus that they may possess heaven and earth, obtaining each by means of the other, To effect this, they continually devise and batch new statutes and new doctrinals. They make the same endeavor also in the other life as they made in the world, for every one after death is such as he was in the world, especially as to his religion. It was granted me to hear certain of the primates consulting about a doctrine, which was to be a rule for the people: it consisted of many articles, but they all tended to this; that they might obtain dominion over the heavens, and the earth, and that they might have all power for themselves, and the Lord none. These doctrinals were after. wards read before the bystanders, and thereupon a voice was heard from heaven, declaring, that they were dictated from the deepest hell, though the hearers did not know it; which was further confirmed by this; that a crowd of devils from that hell, of the blackest and direst appearance, ascended, and tore those doctrinals from them, not with their hands, but with their teeth, and carried them down to their hell. The people who saw it were astounded.

IV. Why they were there tolerated, until the day of the Last Judgment. The reason was, because it is from Divine order that all who can be preserved, shall be preserved, even until they can no longer be among the good. Therefore all those are preserved, who can emulate spiritual life in externals, and present it in a moral life, as if it were therein, whatever they may be as to faith and love in Internals; so also those are preserved who are in external holiness, though not in internal. Such were many of that nation, for they could speak piously with the common people, and adore the Lord in a holy manner to implant religion in their minds, and lead them to think of heaven and hell, and could hold them in doing goods by preaching works. Thus they were able to lead many to a life of good, and therefore into the way to heaven; on which account also, many of that religion were saved, although few of their leaders. For these are such as the Lord means by: False prophets, who come in sheep's clothing, but inwardly are ravening wolves (Matt. 7:15). By "prophets," in the internal sense of the Word, are meant those who teach truth, and by it lead to good; and by "false prophets," those who teach falsity, and seduce by it. They are also like the scribes and Pharisees, who are described by the Lord in these words: They sit in Moses' seat; all things that they bid you observe, observe and do, but do not according to their word; for they say and do not; all their works they do to be seen of men; they shut up the kingdom of the heavens against men, but go not in themselves: they eat widows' houses, for a pretence pouring forth long prayers. Woe unto you, hypocrites, ye make clean the outside of the cup and platter, but within they are full of rapine and iniquity; cleanse first the inside of the cup and platter, that the outside may be clean also; ye are like whited sepulchres, which appear outwardly beautiful, but within are full of the bones of the dead: thus ye outwardly appear just before men, but within ye are full of hypocrisy and iniquity (Matt. 23:1-34). Another reason moreover why they were tolerated was, because every man after death retains his religious principles that he has acquired in the world; into which therefore he is introduced, when first he comes into the other life. Now with this nation, the religious principle was implanted by those who gave an oral preference to sanctity, and feigned holy gestures, and moreover, impressed the people with a belief that they could be saved through them; hence also they were removed, but were preserved among their own. But the principal reason was, that all are preserved from one judgment to another, who live a life similar to a spiritual life in externals, and emulate as it were a pious and holy internal; by whom the simple may receive instruction and guidance: for the simple in faith and heart look no farther than to see what is external, and apparent before the eyes. Hence all such were tolerated from the commencement of the Christian church, until the day of the judgment. That a Last Judgment has existed twice before, and now exists for the third time, was shown above. Of all these "the former heaven" consisted, and they are meant in the Apocalypse (20:5, 6) by "those who are not of the first resurrection." But since they were such as above described, that heaven was destroyed, and they of the second resurrection were cast out. But it ought to be known that they only were preserved who suffered themselves to be held in bonds by laws both civil and spiritual, they being capable of living together in society; nevertheless they who could not be held in bonds by those laws were not preserved, but were cast into hell long before the day of the Last Judgment: for societies are continually purified and purged from such. Hence, they who led a wicked life, who enticed the common people to do evils, and entered on abominable arts, such as exist among spirits in the hells, were cast out of societies, and this in their turns. In like manner also those who are interiorly good are removed from societies, lest they should be contaminated by those who are interiorly evil; for the good perceive the interiors, and therefore pay no regard to the exteriors, except just so far as they agree with the interiors; they are sent in their turns to places of instruction, and are carried thence into heaven; for "the new heaven" is formed of them, and they are meant by "those who are of the first resurrection." These things are said that it may be known, why so many of the Papal religion were tolerated and preserved until the day of the Last Judgment; but more will be said on the same subject in the following article, where "the first heaven" which passed away is to be treated of.

V. How they were destroyed, and their habitations made a desert. This I will here describe in a few words; more fully in the Explanation of the Apocalypse. That Babylonia there treated of has been destroyed, no one but he who saw it can know, and it was given me to see how the Last Judgment was brought about and accomplished upon all, especially upon those of Babylon. I, therefore, will describe it This was granted me, principally, in order to reveal to the world, that all things predicted in the Apocalypse are Divinely inspired, and that the Apocalypse is a prophetic book of the Word. For if this were not revealed to the world, and at the same time the internal sense which is in each expression there, as in each expression of the Prophets of the Old Testament, that book might be rejected, on account of not being understood; which would produce such incredulity, that the things there said would not be held worthy of belief, nor that any such Last Judgment would come; in which unbelief those of the Babylon would confirm themselves more than others. Lest this should be, it pleased the Lord to make me an eye-witness. But all that I saw of the Last Judgment upon those of the Babylon, or of the destruction of Babylon, cannot be here adduced, being in itself sufficient to fill a volume. In this place I shall merely relate certain general things, reserving the particulars for the Explanation of the Apocalypse. Inasmuch as the Babylonish nation was settled in and extended over many tracts in the spiritual world, and had formed to itself societies in all the quarters there, I will describe how they were destroyed separately in each quarter.

Destruction was effected after visitation, for visitation always precedes. The act of exploring what the men are, and moreover the separation of the good from the evil, is visitation; and the good are then removed, and the evil are left behind. This having been done, there were great earthquakes, from which they perceived that the Last Judgment was at hand, and trembling seized them all. Then those who dwelt in the southern quarter, and especially in the great city there, were seen running to and fro, some with the intention of betaking themselves to flight, some of hiding themselves in the crypts, others of hiding in the cells and caves where their treasures were, out of which others again carried anything they could lay their hands on. But after the earthquakes there burst up an ebullition from below, which overturned everything in the city and in the region round it. After this ebullition came a vehement wind from the east which laid bare, shook, and overthrew everything to its foundations, and then all who were there were led forth, from every part, and from all their hiding-places, and cast into a sea of black waters: those who were cast into it, were many myriads. Afterwards from that whole region a smoke ascended, as after a conflagration, and finally a thick dust, which was borne by the east wind to the sea, and strewn over it; for their treasures were turned into dust, with all those things they had called holy because they possessed them. This dust was strewn over the sea, because such dust signifies what is damned. At last there was seen as it were a blackness flying over that whole region, which when it was viewed narrowly appeared like a dragon; a sign that the whole of that great city and region was become a desert, This was seen, because "dragons" signify the falsities of such a religion, and "the abode of dragons" signifies the desert after their overthrow; as in Jeremiah (9:11; x. 22; 49:33; Mal. 1:3) It was also seen that some had as it were a millstone around the left arm, which was a representative of their having confirmed their abominable dogmas from the Word; a millstone signifies such things: hence it was plain what these words signify in the Apocalypse: The angel took up a stone like a great millstone, and cast it into the sea, saying, thus with violence shall that great city Babylon be thrown down, and shall no more be found (Apoc. 18:21). But they who were in the council, which also was in that region, but nearer to the east, in which they were consulting on the modes of enlarging their dominion, and of keeping the people in ignorance, and thence in blind obedience , were not cast into that black sea, but into a gulf which opened itself long and deep beneath and around them. Thus was the Last Judgment accomplished upon the Babylonians in the southern quarter. But the Last Judgment upon those in front in the western quarter, and upon those in the northern quarter, where the other great city stood, was thus effected. After great earthquakes, which rent everything in those quarters to the very foundations-these are the earthquakes which are meant in the Word (Matt. 24:7; Luke 21:11; likewise Apoc. 6:12; 8:5; 11:13; 16:18); and in the prophecies of the Old Testament, and not any earthquakes in this world-an east wind went forth from the south through the west into the north, and laid bare that whole region first that part of it in front in the western quarter, where the people of the dark ages dwelt underground, and afterwards the great city, which extended from that quarter even through the north to the east, and from these regions thus laid bare, all things were exposed to view. But because there were not such great riches there, no ebullition, and no sulphurous fire consuming treasures were seen, but only overturn and destruction, and at length exhalation of the whole into smoke; for the east wind went forth, blowing to and fro; it overthrew and destroyed and also swept away. The monks and common people were led forth to the number of many myriads; some were cast into the black sea, on that side of it which faces the west; some into the great southern gulf, mentioned above; some into the western gulf, and some into the hells of the Gentiles, for a part of those who lived in the dark ages were idolaters like the Gentiles, A smoke also was seen to ascend from that region, and to proceed as far as the sea; over which it hovered, depositing a black crust there; for that part of the sea into which they were cast, was encrusted over with the dust and smoke, into which their dwellings and their riches were reduced; wherefore that sea has no longer a visible existence, but in its place is seen, as it were a black soil, under which is their hell, The Last Judgment upon those who dwelt upon the mountains in the eastern quarter , was thus accomplished. Their mountains were seen to subside into the deep, and all those who were upon them to be swallowed up; and he whom they had placed upon one of the mountains, and whom they proclaimed to be god, was seen to become first black, then fiery, and with them to be cast headlong into hell. For the monks of the various orders who were upon those mountains, said that he was God and that they were Christ, and wherever they went, they took with them the abominable persuasion that themselves were Christ. Finally, judgment was effected upon those who dwelt more remotely in the western quarter, upon the mountains there, and who are meant by "the woman sitting upon the scarlet beast who had seven heads which are seven mountains," of whom also something is related above. Their mountains also were seen, some were open in the middle, where an immense chasm was made and whirled about in a spiral, into which those on the mountains were cast. Other mountains were torn up by their foundations and turned upside down, so that the summit became the base; those who were thence in the plains were inundated as with a deluge, and covered over, and those who were among them from other quarters were cast into gulfs. But the things now related are only a small part of all I saw; more will be given in the Explanation of the Apocalypse. They were effected and accomplished in the beginning of the year 1757. As regards the gulfs into which all were cast, except those who were cast into the black sea, they are many. Four of them were disclosed to me; one great gulf in the southern quarter, towards the east there; another in the western quarter, towards the south; a third in the western quarter, towards the north there; a fourth still further in the angle between the west and the north: the gulfs and the sea are their hells. These were seen, but in addition to these there are many more, which were not seen; for the hells of the Babylonish people are distinct according to the various profanations of spiritual things, which are of the good and truth of the church.

Thus now was the spiritual world freed from such spirits, and the angels rejoiced on account of its liberation from them, because they who were of Babylon infested and seduced all whomsoever they could, and there more than in the world; for their cunning is more malignant there, because they are spirits; for it is the spirit of each in which all his wickedness is hidden, since the spirit of the man is what thinks, wills, intends, and plots. Many of them were explored, and it was found that they believed nothing at all, and that the heinous lust of seducing, the rich for the sake of their riches, and the poor for the sake of dominion, was rooted in their minds, and that on account of that end they kept all in the densest ignorance, thus blocking up the way to light, thus to heaven: for the way to light and to heaven is obstructed, when the knowledges of spiritual things are overwhelmed by idolatries, and when the Word is adulterated, weakened, and taken away.

VI. Those of them who were in the affection of truth from good were preserved. Those of the Papal nation who lived piously, and were in good, although not in truths, and still from affection desired to know truths, were taken away and carried into a certain region, in front in the western quarter, near the north, and there habitations were given them, and societies of them were instituted, and then priests from the Reformed were sent to them, who instructed them from the Word, and as they are instructed, they are accepted in heaven.

The state of those hereafter who come thence from the earth. Since the Last Judgment has now been accomplished, and by means of it all things are reduced by the Lord into order, and since all who are interiorly good are taken into heaven, and all who are interiorly evil are cast into hell, it is not permitted them henceforth as heretofore, to form societies below heaven and above hell, nor to have anything in common with others, but as soon as they come thither, which is after the death of each, they are altogether separated, and after passing a certain time in the world of spirits, they are carried into their own places. They therefore who profane holy things, that is, who claim for themselves the power of opening and shutting heaven, and of remitting sins, which yet are powers belonging to the Lord alone, and who make Papal bulls equal to the Word, and have dominion for an end, are henceforth carried away immediately into that black sea, or into the gulfs, where the hells of profaners are. But it was said to me from heaven, that those of that religious persuasion who are such, do not look at all to the life after death, because they deny it in heart, but only to life in the world; and that hence they hold of no account this lot of theirs after death, which yet is to endure to eternity, but laugh at it, as a thing of nought.

X. THE FORMER HEAVEN AND ITS ABOLISHMENT. It is said in the Apocalypse: I saw a great throne, and One sitting upon it, from whose face the earth and the heaven fled away, and their place was not found (Rev. 20:11). And afterwards: I saw a new heaven and a new earth; the first heaven and the first earth had passed away (Rev. 21:1). That by "a new heaven and a new earth," and by the passing away of the former heaven and the former earth is not meant the visible heaven and our habitable earth, but an angelic heaven and a church, was shown above in the first article, and also in those which follow it. For the Word in itself is spiritual, and therefore treats of spiritual things; and spiritual things are the things of heaven and the church; these are expressed by natural things in the sense of the letter, because natural things serve as a basis to spiritual things, and without such a basis the Word would not be a Divine work, because it would not be complete; for the natural, which is the ultimate in Divine order, completes and makes the interiors, which are spiritual and celestial, to subsist upon it, as a house upon its foundation. Now because man has thought of the things of the Word from the natural and not from the spiritual, therefore, by "the heaven and the earth" which are mentioned here and elsewhere, they have understood none other than the heaven and earth which exist in the world of nature; hence it is that everyone expects the passing away and destruction of these, and then also the creation of new ones. But lest they should expect this everlastingly, from age to age in vain, the spiritual sense of the Word is opened, that thus it may be known what is meant by many things in the Word, which, when thought of naturally, do not enter the understanding, and, at the same time, what is meant by "the heaven and the earth" which will pass away.

But before showing what is meant by "the first heaven and the first earth," it should be known, that by "the first heaven" is not meant the heaven formed of those who have become angels from the first creation of this world to the present time, for that heaven is abiding, and endures to eternity; for all who enter heaven are under the Lord's protection, and he who has once been received by the Lord, can never be plucked away from Him. But by "the first heaven" is meant that which was composed of others than those who have become angels, and for the most part of those who could not become angels. Who they were, and their quality, shall be told in the following pages. This heaven it is, of which it is said, that it "passed away." It was called heaven, because they who were in it dwelt on high, forming societies upon rocks and mountains, and living in delights similar to natural ones, but still not in any that were spiritual; for very many who come from the earth into the spiritual world, believe themselves to be in heaven, when they are on high, and in heavenly joy, when they are in delights such as they had in the world. Hence it wasn't called heaven, but "the first heaven which passed away."

It is moreover to be known, that this heaven which is called "the first," did not consist of any who had lived before the Lord's coming into the world, but all were from those who lived after His coming, for as was shown above a Last Judgment is effected at the end of every church, and then the former heaven is abolished, and a new heaven is created or formed; for all who lived in an external moral life, and in external piety and sanctity, although not in any internal, were tolerated from the beginning to the end of the church provided the internals which belong to the thoughts and intentions could be held in bonds by the laws of society, civil and moral; but at the end of the church their internals are disclosed, and the judgment is then effected upon them, Hence it is that a Last Judgment has been effected upon the inhabitants of this planet twice before, and now for the third time ; thus also a heaven and an earth have twice passed away before, and a new heaven and a new earth have been created; for the heaven and the earth are the church in either world, as shown above. Hence it is plain, that "the new heaven and the new earth," mentioned in the prophets of the Old Testament, are not that "new heaven and new earth" mentioned in the Apocalypse, but that the former existed from the Lord when He was in the world, and that the latter exist from Him now. Concerning those in the prophets of the Old Testament, it is thus written: Behold, I am about to create a new heaven and a new earth, neither shall the former be remembered (Isa. 65:17). And in another place: I am about to make a new heaven and a new earth (Isa. 66:22). Besides what is said in Daniel.

Since the first heaven which passed away is the subject now treated of, and since no one knows anything concerning it, I will describe it in order. I. Of whom the first heaven consisted. II. What its quality was. III. How it passed away.

I. Of whom the first heaven consisted. The first heaven was composed of all those upon whom the Last Judgment was effected, for it was not effected upon those in hell, nor upon those in heaven, nor upon those in the world of spirits, concerning which world see the work on Heaven and Hell (n. 421-520), nor upon any man yet living, but solely upon those who had made to themselves the likeness of a heaven, of whom the greater part were on mountains and rocks; these also were they whom the Lord meant by "the goats," which He placed on the left (Matt. 25:32, 33, seq.). Hence it may appear, that the first heaven existed, not merely from Christians, but also from Mohammedans and Gentiles, who had all formed to themselves such heavens in their own places. What their quality was shall be told in a few words. They were those who had lived in the world in external and not in internal holiness; who were just and sincere for the sake of civil and moral laws, but not for the sake of Divine laws, therefore who were external or natural and not internal or spiritual men; who also were in the doctrinals of the church, and were able to teach them, although they were not in a life according to them; and who filled various offices, and did uses, but not for the sake of uses. These, and all throughout the whole world who were like them, and who lived after the Lord's coming, constituted "the first heaven." This heaven therefore was such as the world and church is upon earth, among those who do good not because it is good, but because they fear the laws, and the loss of fame, honor, and gain; they who do good for no other origin, do not fear God, but men, nor do they have any conscience. In the first heaven of the Reformed, there was a large part of them, who believed that man is saved by faith alone, and had not lived the life of faith, which is charity; and who loved much to be seen of men. In all these, so long as they were associated together, the interiors were closed that they might not appear, but when the Last Judgment was at hand they were opened; and it was then found that inwardly they were obsessed by falsities and evils of every kind, and that they were against the Divine, and were actually in hell For every one after death is immediately bound to his like, the good to their like in heaven, but the evil to their like in hell, yet they do not go to them before the interiors are disclosed; in the meantime they may be consociated with those who are like them in externals. But it is to be known that all who were interiorly good thus who were spiritual, were separated from them, and elevated into heaven, and that all who were exteriorly as well as interiorly evil, were also separated from them, and cast into hell; and this from the time immediately succeeding the Lord's advent, down to the last time, when the judgment was; and that those only were left, to form societies among themselves, who constituted the first heaven, and who were such as are described above,

There were many reasons why such societies, or such heavens were tolerated; the principal reason was, that by external holiness, and by external sincerity and justice, they were conjoined with the simple good, who were either in the lowest heaven, or were still in the world of spirits and not yet introduced into heaven. For in the spiritual world, there is a communication, and thence a conjunction, of all with their like; and the simple good, in the lowest heaven, and in the world of spirits, look principally to externals, yet are not interiorly evil; wherefore if these spirits had been forcibly removed from them before the appointed time, heaven would have suffered in its ultimates; and yet it is the ultimate, upon which the superior heaven subsists, as upon its own basis. That they were tolerated until the last time on this account, the Lord teaches in the following words: The servants of the householder came and said unto him, Didst thou not sow good seed in thy field, whence then are the tares? And they said, Wilt thou then that we go and gather them up? But he said, Nay, lest, whilst ye gather up the tares, ye root up at the same time the wheat with them; let both therefore grow together until the harvest, and at the time of harvest I will say to the reapers, gather ye together first the tares, and bind them in bundles to burn; but gather the wheat into barns. He that hath sowed the good seed, is the Son of man; the field is the world; the good seed are the sons of the kingdom, the tares are the sons of evil; the harvest is the consummation of the age: as therefore the tares are gathered together, and burnt with fire, so shall it be in the consummation of the age (Matt, 13:27-30, 37-40). "The consummation of this age," is the last time of the church; "the tares" are those who are interiorly evil; "the wheat" are those who are interiorly good; "the gathering the tares together, and binding them in bundles to burn," is the Last Judgment. The like is meant in the same chapter by the Lord's parable of the fishes of every kind, which were gathered together, and the good placed in vessels, but the bad cast away; concerning which it is also said: So shall it be in the consummation of the age; the angels shall go forth, and separate the evil from the midst of the just (vers. 47-49). They are compared to fishes, because "fishes" in the spiritual sense of the Word, signify natural and external men, both good and evil; what "the just" signify may be seen below. "Bundles" in the Word signify the arrangement of the truths and falsities with man into series, thus also the arrangement of men in whom truths and falsities are. "The Son of man" is the Lord as to Divine truths. "Sons" are the affections of truth from good ; therefore "the sons of the kingdom" are those who are in the affections of truth from good; and "the sons of evil," those who are in the affections of falsity from evil; whence the latter are called tares," and the former "good seed," for "tares" signify falsity from evil, and "good seed," truth from good; "the seed of the field" is truth from good, in man, from the Lord. "Seed" in the opposite sense is falsity from evil. "The seed of the field" is also the nutrition of the mind by Divine truth from the Word and "sowing" is instruction. "The consummation of the age" is the last time of the church."Fishes," in the spiritual sense of the Word, signify scientifics, which belong to the natural or external man, and hence also natural or external men, both evil and good. Animals of all kinds correspond with such things as are with man. In the Word, they to whom the Lord's justice and merit are attributed, are called "just"; they to whom their own justice and merit are attributed, are called "unjust".

II. What the quality of the first heaven was, may be concluded from the things already said of it; as also from this, that they who are not spiritual by acknowledgment of the Divine, by a life of good, and by the affection of truth, and still appear as spiritual by external holiness, by discoursing on Divine things, and by sincerities for the sake of themselves and the world, rush into the abominations which agree with their lusts, when they are left to their own internals; for nothing withholds them, neither fear of God, nor faith, nor conscience. Hence it was, that as soon as they who were in the first heaven were let into their interiors, they appeared conjoined with the hells.

III. How the first heaven passed away, was described before, in describing the Last Judgment upon the Mohammedans and Gentiles ; and upon the Papists , since they also in their own places were constituents of the first heaven, It remains that something be said of the Last Judgment upon the Reformed, who are also called Protestants and Evangelical, or how the first heaven composed of them passed away; for, as was said above, judgment was effected upon those only of whom the first heaven consisted, After being visited, and let into their own interiors, they were separated from each other, and divided into classes according to evils and falsities therefrom, and according to falsities and evils therefrom, and were cast into hells corresponding to their loves. Their hells surrounded the middle region on all sides, for the Reformed were in the middle, the Papists around them, the Mohammedans around the Papists, and the Gentiles in the outmost circuit. Those who were not cast into hells, were cast out into deserts; but there were some sent down to the plains in the southern and northern quarters, there to form societies, and be instructed and prepared for heaven; these are they who were preserved. But how all these things were accomplished, cannot be described in particular in this place, for the judgment upon the Reformed was of longer continuance than upon others, and was effected by successive changes. Now since much that is worthy of mention was then heard and seen, I will present the particulars in their own order in the Explanation of the Apocalypse.

XI. THE STATE OF THE WORLD AND OF THE CHURCH HEREAFTER. The state of the world hereafter will be altogether similar to what it has been heretofore, for the great change which has taken place in the spiritual world, does not induce any change in the natural world as to the external form; so that after this there will be civil affairs as before, there will be peace, treaties, and wars as before, with all other things which belong to societies in general and in particular, The Lord said that: In the last times there will be wars, and then nation will rise against nation, and kingdom against kingdom, and there will be famines, pestilences, and earthquakes in divers places (Matt. 24:6, 7). This does not signify that such things will exist in the natural world, but that the things corresponding with them will exist in the spiritual world: for the Word in its prophecies does not treat of the kingdoms on earth, nor of the nations there, thus neither concerning their wars, nor of famines, pestilences, and earthquakes there, but of such things as correspond to them in the spiritual world; what these things are, is explained in the Arcana Coelestia, and a collection of passages on the subject may be seen below. But as for the state of the church, this it is which will be dissimilar hereafter; it will be similar indeed as to the external appearance, but dissimilar as to the internal. As to the external appearance divided churches will exist as heretofore, their doctrines will be taught as heretofore; and the same religions as now will exist among the Gentiles. But henceforth the man of the church will be in a more free state of thinking on matters of faith, thus on the spiritual things which relate to heaven, because spiritual freedom has been restored to him. For all things in the heavens and in the hells are now reduced into order, and all thought concerning Divine things and against the Divine inflows from thence; from the heavens all thought which is in harmony with Divine things, and from the hells all which is against Divine things. But man does not observe this change of state in himself, because he does not reflect upon it, and because he knows nothing of spiritual freedom and of influx; nevertheless it is perceived in heaven, and also by man himself after his death. Because spiritual freedom has been restored to man, therefore the spiritual sense of the Word has now been disclosed, and by it interior Divine truths have been revealed; for man in his former state would not have understood them, and he who would have understood them, would have profaned them. That man has freedom by means of the equilibrium between heaven and hell, and, that man cannot be reformed except in freedom, may be seen in the work on Heaven and Hell. That "wars" in the Word signify spiritual combats. Hence all "the arms of war," as "the bow," "the sword," "the shield," signify something of spiritual combat. "Kingdoms" signify churches as to truths and as to falsities. "Nations" signify those in the church who are in goods and who are in evils. "Famine" signifies a defect of the knowledges of good and truth. It also signifies the desolation of the church. "Pestilence" signifies the vastation and consummation of good and truth. "Earthquakes" signify changes of the state of the church.

I have had various conversations with angels, concerning the state of the church hereafter. They said that they know not things to come, for the knowledge of things to come belongs to the Lord alone; but they know that the slavery and captivity in which the man of the church was formerly, has been taken away, and that now, from restored freedom, he can better perceive interior truths, if he wills to perceive them; and thus be made more internal, if he wills to become so; but that still they have slender hope of the men of the Christian church, but much of some nation far distant from the Christian world, and therefore removed from infesters, which nation is such that it is capable of receiving spiritual light, and of being made a celestial-spiritual man, and they said, that at this day interior Divine truths are revealed in that nation, and are also received in spiritual faith, that is, in life and heart, and that they adore the Lord.

www.ingramcontent.com/pod-product-compliance
Lightning Source LLC
Chambersburg PA
CBHW031656040426
42453CB00006B/323